Business Analysis and Process Modeling Guidebook

Business Analysis Techniques and Business Process Improvement

Copyright © 2022 by RKA Press.

All rights reserved. No part of this publication may be reproduced, distributed, or transmitted in any form or by any means, including photocopying, recording, or other electronic or mechanical methods, without the prior written permission of the publisher, except in the case of brief quotations embodied in critical reviews and specific other noncommercial uses permitted by copyright law.

No warranty

This book material provided "as-is." The writer offers no warranties of any kind, either expressed or implied, as to any matter including, but not limited to, warranty of fitness for purpose or merchantability, exclusivity, or results obtained from the use of the material.

Business Analysis and Process Modeling Guidebook: Business Analysis Techniques and Business Process Improvement

First Edition. (2022)

Use of any trademarks in this book is not intended in any way to infringe on the rights of the trademark holder.

Contents

- **LIST OF FIGURES** 7
- **LIST OF TABLES** 9
- **CHAPTER 1: INTRODUCTION** 11
  - WHAT IS BUSINESS ANALYSIS? 11
  - WHY DOES A PROJECT FAIL? 12
  - THE BUSINESS ANALYST'S ROLE 12
  - SERVICE ECONOMY 13
  - HOW TO IMPROVE BUSINESS 15
  - DEFINE PROBLEM STATEMENT 17
- **CHAPTER 2: STRATEGY ANALYSIS AND BENEFITS REALIZATION** 19
  - BUSINESS STRATEGY 20
  - BENEFITS ROAD MAP 24
  - BUSINESS IMPACT ANALYSIS 26
  - RISK ANALYSIS 28
  - PROJECT PRIORITIES 29
  - COST-BENEFIT ANALYSIS 29
  - KEY PERFORMANCE INDICATOR (KPI) 31
  - VALUE CHAIN ANALYSIS 32
  - VALUE PROPOSITION ANALYSIS 33
  - RESPONSIBILITY MATRIX 35
- **CHAPTER 3: FROM OBJECTIVES TO BENEFITS** 37
  - BUSINESS AGILITY 37
  - PROJECT DELIVERY METHODOLOGY 38
  - PORTFOLIO MANAGEMENT 40
  - PROGRAM MANAGEMENT 44
  - PROJECT MANAGEMENT 45
- **CHAPTER 4: ENABLE THE CHANGE** 47
  - WHAT IS A TEAM? 47
  - STAGES OF TEAM DEVELOPMENT 48
  - CONFLICT RESOLUTION AND MANAGEMENT 50
  - ORGANIZATION CHANGE 53
  - ORGANIZATION DEVELOPMENT 54
  - RESISTANCE TO CHANGE 55
- **CHAPTER 5: BUSINESS CASE** 59

| What Is a Business Case? | 59 |
| How to Build a Business Case | 60 |

CHAPTER 6: REQUIREMENTS AND STAKEHOLDERS 63

Define Business Problems	63
Collecting Requirements	64
Stakeholders	65
Prepare for the Meeting	67
Categorize Features	73
Requirement Refinement and Verification	75
Decision Tables	77
Collecting Requirements in Agile Teams	78

CHAPTER 7: BUSINESS PROCESS MODELING 81

| Understanding the Process | 82 |
| Discover and Draw the Current Services | 84 |

CHAPTER 8: PROCESS ASSESSMENT AND STANDARDIZATION 97

Step 1: Initial Plan for the Assessment	100
Step 2: Assemble the Team	102
Step 3: Executing the Plan	103
Generate Results	108
Final Results	116
Remediation	117

CHAPTER 9: PROCESS IMPROVEMENT 119

What Is Process Improvement?	119
Statistical Process Control (SPC)	121
Quality	122
Cost	125
Time	126
Adjusting the Position	128
Understanding Process Outcomes	130
Six Sigma	135

CHAPTER 10: PROCESS AS A STRATEGIC ASSET 141

Step 1: Identify the Process Type and Levels	141
Step 2: Define the Critical Path	142
Step 3: Give Weight to the Steps	144
Step 4: Build Service Maps	144
Step 5: Shorten the Chain	145
Step 6: Make Use of Robots	146

List of figures

Figure 1: Transformation Triangle 14
Figure 2: SWOT Example 21
Figure 3: Goals and Objectives 23
Figure 4: Departments Plans and Objectives Example 23
Figure 5: Benefits Map Example 26
Figure 6: Risk Categories 28
Figure 7: Value Chains 32
Figure 9: Service Value 34
Figure 10: Waterfall Project 38
Figure 11: Agile Project 39
Figure 12: Backlog Chart Example 39
Figure 13: Portfolio Levels 40
Figure 14: Top-down Approach 41
Figure 15: Bottom-up Approach 42
Figure 16: The Hybrid Approach 42
Figure 17: Unfreezing and Refreezing 55
Figure 18: Fishbone Diagram 61
Figure 19: Stakeholder Map 72
Figure 20: Requirements in Agile 79
Figure 21: Story Map 79
Figure 22: Process Evolution 81
Figure 23: Factory 83
Figure 24: Context Diagram Example 88
Figure 25: PDFD Example 89
Figure 26: LDFD 91
Figure 27: Process Levels 94
Figure 29: Completed Swimlane Flowchart, Page 1 95
Figure 30: Completed Swimlane Flowchart, Page 2 96
Figure 31: Completed Swimlane Flowchart, Page 3 96
Figure 32: Standardized vs. Unstandardized Process 98
Figure 33: Master Process 110
Figure 34: Moving through the Levels 113
Figure 35: Activity Chain 120
Figure 36: QCT Triangle 121

Figure 37: Prevention Cost/Time 123
Figure 38: Failure Cost 123
Figure 39: Prevention Cost/Time & Failure Cost 124
Figure 40: Golden and Gray Zones 124
Figure 41: Quality Score 125
Figure 42: Cost Score 126
Figure 43: Task Duration 126
Figure 44: Time Score 127
Figure 45: Intersection Point 127
Figure 46: Position 128
Figure 47: Perfect Scenario 130
Figure 48: Type 1 (No Grouping of Results) 131
Figure 49: Type 2 (Results Grouped) 131
Figure 50: Statistical Process Control (median moving range-MMR) 132
Figure 51: Process Ranges 133
Figure 52: Quality Circle Concept 133
Figure 53: Data Points 134
Figure 54: Normal Distribution 134
Figure 55: SPC Chart 139
Figure 56: Process Types 142
Figure 57: Process Map 143
Figure 58: Process Critical Map 143
Figure 59: Process Contribution 144
Figure 60: Process Owners 145
Figure 61: Process Split 146

List of tables

Table 1: SWOT Analysis 21
Table 2: Objectives Weight Example 23
Table 3: Tangible and Intangible Example 27
Table 4: Cost Ratios 30
Table 5: Responsibility Matrix Roles 35
Table 6: RACI Matrix Example 35
Table 7: Project Selection and Prioritization 43
Table 8: Team Types 47
Table 9: Team Members' Roles 48
Table 10: Stakeholder Example 65
Table 11: Stakeholder Table Map Example 72
Table 12: Communication Plan Example 73
Table 13: Requirements Traceability Matrix Example 74
Table 14: Decision Table Example 78
Table 15: Activities List Example 86
Table 16: Diagram Shapes 87
Table 17: LDFD Groups 90
Table 18: Flowchart Symbols 92
Table 19: Evidence Sheet Example 104
Table 20: Categorized Evidence Sheet Example..104
Table 21: Service-to-evidence Mapping Example 105
Table 22: Collected Evidence Table Example 107
Table 23: Service Levels 109
Table 24 Process Distribution 142
Table 25 Move the Process 146

Chapter 1: Introduction

In this book, business analysis concepts are linked together, and mixed with project management, necessary business skills, and hands-on experience. The book is a road map for anyone interested in business analysis process modeling and improvement. The readership for this book also includes beginners interested in gaining knowledge about the business analysis process.

This book has two main parts. The first part (chapters 1 through 7) talks about the business analysis process and how to gather and manage the business requirements, translate them into business objectives, and build the process maps. The second part (chapters 8, 9, 10, and 11) discusses business process optimization and improvement. Each chapter covers a topic. However, each chapter also stands alone for easier reference later. The chapters create a road map to help readers understand the role of a project in an organization, remove organizational obstacles and resistance to change, gather and manage requirements, build the process, and optimize and improve the process.

What Is Business Analysis?

Business analysis is the practice of controlling organizational changes to achieve required goals and objectives by using requirement engineering. Requirement engineering is the practice of mapping and transforming stakeholder requirements into a technical statement.

Sound business analysis can help ensure that any project or initiative within an organization can create value and help achieve company objectives.

Process modeling within the business analysis is the practice of documenting and mapping the process to achieve business objectives with maximum efficiency. It used to be present in the process only in graphical format. But the role has evolved into modeling and engineering.

Why Does a Project Fail?

A project is a change attempt in the organization to achieve a specific outcome. Projects fail for many reasons, but the most common are these:

- Lack of stakeholder engagement and involvement
- Changing priorities and failure to manage those changes properly
- Changing requirements
- Inaccurate requirements
- Uninvolved sponsors
- Changing project objective
- Inaccurate project estimates
- An unexpected risk that cannot be mitigated
- Dependencies
- Inadequate resources
- Scope creep (adding scope without considering the impact on resources and schedule)

Most of the reasons reflect a failure in planning or in collecting what the project is trying to accomplish. And that falls directly into the business analyst's roles and responsibilities.

The Business Analyst's Role

A business analyst's role is to take a considerable task/problem/requirement/project and turn it into small, easily understood requirements and objectives. When all requirements are combined, the big picture becomes clear to everyone.

A business analyst does this breakdown by identifying the organization's needs through requirement-gathering techniques and by working with a subject matter expert (SME) to create solutions to a business problem.

The business analyst's role is separate from that of the project manager, who is responsible primarily for delivering the work of the project on time and within budget.

The business analyst, by contrast, is responsible for ensuring the project meets specified requirements that deliver company value.

Business Analysis Techniques and Business Process Improvement | 13

The business analyst's role is not a technical role. The core business analyst's role is to do the following:

- Validate organization objectives and processes to achieve the proposed project
- Manage the requirement process using flowcharts, user stories, and context diagrams
- Manage any change and make sure the organization and the project are aligned
- Manage the testing and make sure the outcomes align with project goals
- Ensure that all project objectives are achieved

There are several scopes the business analysis should focus on:

- The project activities and securing the necessary resources
- The value that must be achieved on behalf of the end user
- The functions that must be delivered in each area of the activities
- The technical aspects of all functions within the project scope

Role Variations

It used to be one business analyst doing all the things, but now the role responsibilities are getting more demanding, requiring specializations within the role. All the roles should know how to collect requirements with additional expertise in these areas:

- Process modeling
- Agile (product owner)
- Application prototyping and design
- Data analyst (industry-specific)

This book aims to provide core business analysis knowledge and an understanding of the process modeling specialization.

Service Economy

Service is a value delivered to the end customer. Without the resulting value, the service is useless.

Think about a restaurant that provides both in-house food service and catering. If the food is excellent, but the waiters are unprofessional, imagine the restaurant's bottom-line consequences. Likewise, if vegetables are good but the meat is undercooked, owners can expect customer dissatisfaction and a decline in business.

There are always three main factors in any transformation: people, processes, and technology. Focus on a single factor in each project. If the focus is on multiple factors simultaneously, the project will have difficulty achieving the expected result and might fail.

- **People**: how to change attitudes and mindset, and influence organizational culture
- **Process**: how to implement a new process or adjust the current one
- **Technology**: how to select the correct tools that will fit the purpose

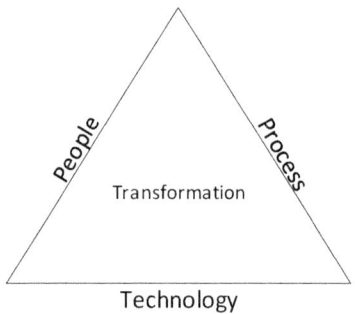

Figure 1: Transformation Triangle

The general concept now is that all businesses are service businesses, even those that sell specific physical products. Comparing this with the SaaS economy that is emerging will lead to more focus on the business's services. Some even say there are no customers any longer, only subscribers, which leads to a constant analysis process.

The main challenge for a business analyst is to orchestrate all of the benefits expected from a project to impact the three verticals of people, process, and technology simultaneously.

How to Improve Business

To improve the business, you need to improve the services provided by the business, either internal services or external services. Among the goals may be reducing costs and risks, improving satisfaction and flexibility, and delivering new services through new channels.

In today's dynamic and competitive business environment, organizations must constantly adjust operations to meet market challenges and to gain a competitive edge.

Improvement Opportunities:

These are standard or quick wins that you should consider whenever you draw a process or become part of a project:

- **The repetitive process**: Unify any process that coexists with similar activities into one process.
- **Conflict in the process**: Evaluate any process that conflicts with another for possible elimination.
- **Unneeded processes**: Consider resolving or eliminating any process that hasn't been used or is outdated.
- **Reduction of manual labor**: Automating tasks reduces the risk of human error. Automation will allow teams to focus more effectively on critical areas instead of waiting to put out fires and performing repetitive actions. This will allow teams to deliver greater end-user satisfaction.
- **Cost reduction**: Any organization is created for a purpose—to generate cash flow (for profit) or to provide aid and support (nonprofit). Reducing a for-profit company's costs improves the bottom line. Similarly, reducing a nonprofit organization's cost can enhance its ability to provide aid and support.
- **Insight into problem areas**: Discover areas that should be marked for improvement.
- **Reduction of wasted time**: Eliminating waste can bolster a bottom line.
- **Proper budget planning**: Improving operations can give a business a clearer sense of where to allocate spending.

- **Better overview of how an organization functions**: A clearer picture of business operations can enhance the bottom line and increase stakeholder satisfaction.

Common Technology Trends

When gathering requirements, it helps to have some ideas about areas for improvement. Knowledge of current technology trends will drive more in-depth conversations with the stakeholders.

- **Natural language generation (NLG)**: Artificial intelligence (AI) automates data into human-readable text. In such a solution, the business analyst needs to assess the outcome and provide guidance on how to enhance it.
- **Speech recognition**: This is the ability to translate spoken words into text.
- **Voice systems (auto-attendant)**: This is the capability for human-like interaction.
- **Chatbot:** This is a customer service voice simulation tool inside an app or website. In this solution, the business analyst needs to gather scenarios and continue updating the voice response possibilities, escalating to a human when needed. Chatbots are not limited to chatting. They can respond to emails or simple calls.
- **Process automation**: This series of steps mimics human interactions.
- **Machine learning**: In this solution, the computer learns patterns on its own without the need to feed it scenarios. Humans correct any deviations, and those corrections are fed into the learning process. Machine learning is beneficial in analyzing a large volume of data and creating what-if scenarios.

Though these are just definitions, you should be on the lookout for areas that fall within these technologies with each project.

Define Problem Statement

In any engagement, the starting point is defining its driver, in other words, the problem statement. Without the business driver, this project will lack management support, leading to project failure. So defining the problem early on helps eliminate this risk.

The problem statement should be clear and precise and should focus on a specific issue that you intend to address through the project. The problem statement should be relevant from a managerial perspective.

Almost any type of service needs some improvement. As long as an organization exists, some of its most common needs are the ability to address the following:

- Dissatisfied stakeholders
- Projects with scope creep
- Missed requirements

The goal is to improve the business, for example, by enhancing customer satisfaction.

You might face many gains from solving a particular problem. Try to focus on only one or two benefits and give them full attention. This focus will accelerate the projects by limiting the number of sponsors. All other parties will be included as critical later on in the stakeholder definition. Don't try to go big bang and change the entire organization all at once.

Avoid analysis paralysis. This is the condition in which the analysis and requirements gathering phase is never over. Always define the goals and success criteria at the start.

Chapter 2: Strategy Analysis and Benefits Realization

Business benefits can help an organization achieve its objectives. Typically a series of changes to an organization can be implemented through individual projects. These changes generate outcomes and values. Multiple values from one or more projects, in turn, generate the business benefits. Benefits management begins by identifying the aligned value of these factors:

- The portfolio: all the projects, and the in-progress programs to achieve organization objectives, bridging the gap between strategy and implementation
- The program: a group of projects related to one another and considered a critical part of the portfolio
- The project: a single-purpose objective

A critical part of realizing business objectives is the business analyst's role, with the primary responsibility of identifying the requirements for moving from the current organizational state to the target state.

It is critical to understand that available resources typically are not adequate to satisfy an entire portfolio in any given organization. A selection process is needed. The selection process is part of portfolio management, and the business analyst contributes significantly. Project selection is based on the highest value outcome. All business benefits must be measurable. All objectives must

- be specific.
- have ownership.
- have a process.
- have a plan.
- be traceable.

The business analyst's role is to create the map between the project's five objective elements and link the project to the organization's desired value.

Business Strategy

The business goals For-profit goals are to increase revenue. Nonprofit organizations seek to provide aid and support. To determine the business objective, use one of the following methods.

Business Environment Analysis

The internal environment is the environment that the business controls. The external business environment is everything else, and it represents what the company cannot control. There are multiple analysis models to generate business objectives; the most common is the SWOT analysis. (SWOT stands for strengths, weaknesses, opportunities, and threats.)

SWOT Analysis as Objectives Generator

A SWOT analysis is used for these purposes:

- Conducting an objective analysis of a company
- Determining competitive advantages
- Determining liabilities

Start by identifying the strengths, weaknesses, opportunities, and threats that exist for the organization.

Internal strengths are things the organization does very well. (Examples are a lower-cost operation or a skilled workforce.)

Internal weaknesses are things that are not optimal within the organization. (Examples are poor customer service and negative brand recognition.)

External opportunities are changes external to the organization that could be areas for growth. (For example, a major competitor shuts down, government regulations are relaxed, or technology is updated.)

External threats are changes to the external environment that may negatively impact the organization. (Examples are new technology or increased trade barriers.)

Strengths (internal)	Weaknesses (internal)
S1. Lower cost	W1. Poor customer services
S2. Skilled workforce	W2. Negative quality brand recognition
Opportunities (external)	**Threats (external)**
O1. A major competitor is shutting down	T1. New technology
O2. New relaxed government regulation	T2. Increased trade barriers
O3. New technology	

Figure 2: SWOT Example

Next, matching strengths with weaknesses utilizing brainstorming techniques. Some items will not produce a positive result that can be planned to improve the business. For example, Matching S1 (lower cost) to W1 (poor customer service) will fail, but matching S1 (lower cost) to W2 (negative quality brand recognition) might help in rebranding into an economy brand. Find all possible positive results out of SWOT.

(This is just an example. The analysis below does not include all the possibilities.)

Advantage	Liability
S1.W2 Enhance our marketing to advertise as an economy brand.	**W1.O1** New customers will not desire to work with us and will try to find another alternative.
S2.W1 Train the workforce to serve better.	
S2.W2 Train the workforce to present more of the new message of the friendly economy brand.	**W2.T2.** Our revenue will decrease due to the negative brand recognition locally and trade barriers internationally.
S1.O1. Concentrate the advertising campaign in the area the competitor was working on, showing our product as an alternative.	
S1.T2 Open a branch in a new country with unrestricted trade barriers.	
S1.O1 Open web store.	

Table 1: SWOT Analysis

How the process works

Step 1: All "lines of business" receive their organizational goals and strategy, decide on each objective, and prepare to modify existing systems to achieve each objective. Thus, projects are required. Leaders of each team submit proposed projects designed to meet the objectives.

Step 2: A list of proposals is completed. At this stage, each team presents a business case for pursuing the desired modifications but does not yet have a charter (green light) to go forward. A business analyst can help the team leader build the business case.

For simplicity, an example of a single goal might be handed down from a company board of directors aiming to fulfill its commitment to shareholders. In this case, the stated goal could be to increase profits tenfold this year.

Step 3: To tackle the goal, start by developing tactics that, when combined, will achieve specific objectives. Objectives, in turn, are the small building blocks that constitute the goal. Here is how this might be expressed in the goal of the tenfold profit increase.

- Goal: Increase profit by ten times
- Objectives:
    - Increase customer satisfaction by 10 percent
    - Improve staff morale by 5 percent
    - Increase market share by 2 percent
    - Reduce cost by 10 percent
    - Increase sales by 10 percent

Staff morale and customer satisfaction are typically measured using surveys.

Please note that each of the objectives is scaled from 1 to 10. This scales to reach the desired objective and has a measurement associated with it, which is used in tracking achievement milestones. Example:

- Increase sales by 1 percent
- Increase sales by 2 percent

Business Analysis Techniques and Business Process Improvement | 23

- Increase sales by 3 percent
- ...

Each objective is weighted as well.

Objective	Weight
Increase customer satisfaction 10%	14%
Improve staff morale 5%	11%
Increase market share 2%	37%
Reduce cost by 10%	4%
Increase sales 10%	34%

Table 2: Objectives Weight Example

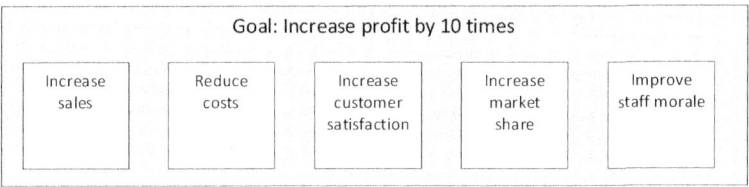

Figure 3: Goals and Objectives

Next, prepare tactics to achieve the selected objectives.

Each line manager begins to think about achieving part or all of the objectives. Some objectives may be shared among multiple business units, and some may be fully executed within a single business unit.

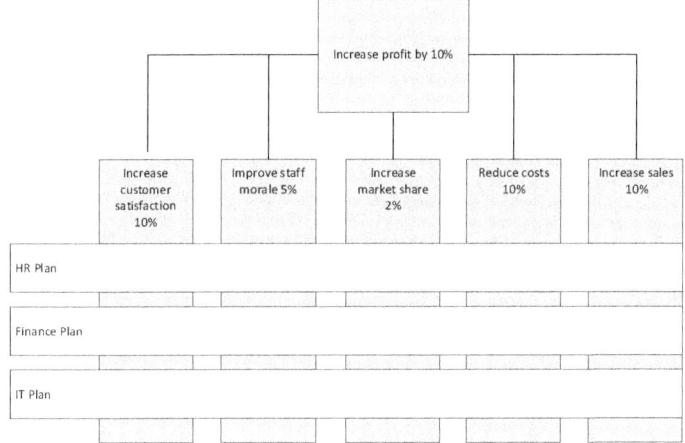

Figure 4: Departments Plans and Objectives Example

To begin, all leaders should submit a business case explaining what tactics they will use to reach an objective. (Depending on team size, a leader may collect ideas and cases from line managers.)

After collecting all ideas and proposed projects, the organization should have a vision of what needs to be changed during the year to achieve the preset goal. And to avoid losing this vision, the organization needs to create the benefits road map.

Benefits Road Map

Start prioritizing projects coming from all plans across all business units to determine the maximum gain for an organization to achieve its goal within its resource constraints. This process is called portfolio analysis. Portfolio management will be discussed later in this book. Project benefits are what an organization uses to justify starting a new project. To build the road map, you need the following:

- **Management support**: This is the sponsor of the project.
- **Expected benefits road map**: This is a high-level picture of the needs of the project.
- **Business benefits realization plan**: To realize the benefits of these programs, a project is created.
- **Measurement of the benefits**: It is preferable to use a dashboard (software or a static webpage) to show overall progress of all projects and benefits.
- **Description of the plan in business format**: This should be summarized and to the point.
- **Explanation of need**: Explain why the project is needed, what it will do for the company, and how it will be accomplished.

Benefits Plan

This single document maps all the benefits from all the projects. All plans must be workable, manageable, and measurable. If a benefit cannot be measured, the organization cannot determine whether a goal has been achieved. The benefits plan should answer these questions:

- What benefits are included?
- How are they measured?
- Who is the sponsor of the project?
- How are benefits monitored?

All benefits collected from stakeholders should be S.M.A.R.T.

- Specific
- Measurable
- Achievable
- Relevant
- Timely

Plan Sections

- Program description
- Scope
- Project vision and objectives
- Project benefits
- Benefits list
- Measured benefits
- Assumptions and risks
- Roles and responsibilities
- Monitoring processes (governance)

You can create a matrix with most of these items shown as a visual aid. The report will help close the project and help show that the value delivered equals the value expected.

Benefits Map

The benefits map shows the relationships among the project's outcomes, program requirements, and organizational goals.

Start from the primary goal, mapping the way to the business benefit.

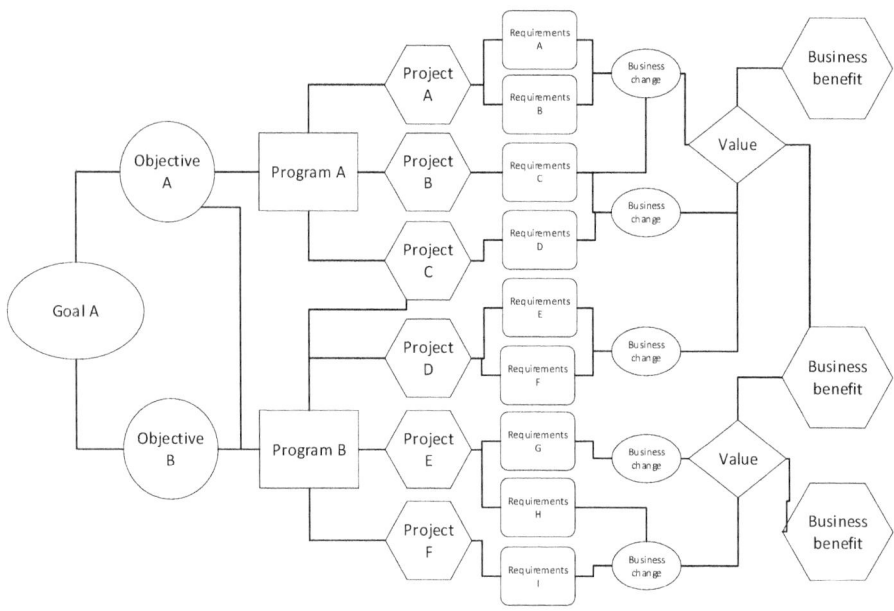

Figure 5: Benefits Map Example

Usually, this map is built once as a visual aid of the relations between goals, projects, requirements, and delivered benefits. After the project starts, updating this map isn't easy. Luckily, almost all project management servers (not the desktop versions) have some interdependencies that map projects to requirements and objectives. This will help to monitor the progress of value realization.

Business Impact Analysis

Another tool to measure the project's importance is the business impact analysis. How much would it cost if operations were interrupted? This is one of the most challenging areas to calculate. In many cases, company confidentiality precludes a business analyst's access to information such as hourly wages, exact website orders and costs, customer loyalty data, and so on. When such information is not available, the impact of operations interruption will be calculated more broadly.

Remember, the business impact analysis measures the overall financial consequences of interruption and is not limited to the effects on just one department. This is why financial information, not technical, guides the process. Associate a price tag with every component and dependency.

The Cost of Failure

The cost of failure is the first component you need to measure. To calculate the cost of failure, use both tangible and intangible costs.

Tangible costs are easily measured and can be associated and discovered directly.

Intangible costs typically are harder to measure and may be deduced through indirect means.

Here are some examples:

Problem	Consequence
Tangible	
Lost user productivity	Paid hours lost
Lost IT staff productivity	Time to resolve the issue
Lost revenue	Revenue lost due to failure
Overtime payments	The team time spent solving the issue
Wasted goods and materials	Materials lost due to failures
Imposed fines	Costs increased
Intangible	
Loss of customers	Decline in sales
Loss of customer satisfaction	Due to failure, customer satisfaction is lower
Loss of business opportunity	Some customers may go to a competitor
Damage to business reputation	Decline in revenue
Loss of confidence in IT provider	Increasing the risks and cost of risk strategy
Damage to staff morale	Loss of trust in their own product

Table 3: Tangible and Intangible Example

After identifying problems and consequences that might impact the project, move to risk analysis to determine the likelihood of a problem materializing.

Risk Analysis

It is crucial to understand both the risks and the impacts of any change.

Risk can be categorized based on probability and impact. Using the X/Y axis, we end up with four risk categories.

Impact can be quantified as the number of losses.

Risk Types

- High probability/high impact
- High probability/low impact
- Low probability/high impact
- Low probability/low impact

To calculate the risk mitigation budget, multiply impact by probability. Always assume there is an unknown risk and arrange a budget for it. Sometimes it's called business risk.

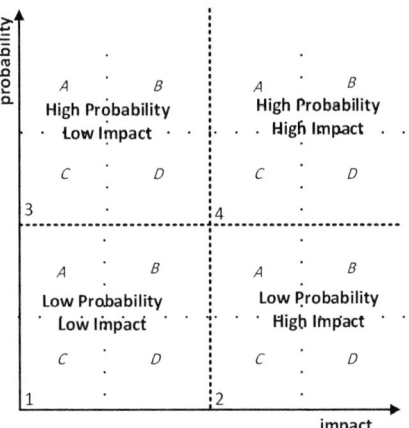

Figure 6: Risk Categories

After determining the issues and the risk associated with a project, move to both probability and impact.

For example, the probability can be a range from 1 to 10, with 10 meaning it's certain and 1 meaning it's highly improbable. For the impact, place a range from 1 to 5 where 5 is a significant loss in business, and 1 is an impact on business image.

Present the information in table format with probability and impact multiplied to generate the risk score. Arrange all risks to prioritize the ones the project manager should consider.

Project Priorities

At this point, you have a list of issues, a list of impacts, and the likelihood. Armed with this, recommend the most likely project to counter the mentioned risks first. Not only that, but changes take priority based on the maintenance windows. And most of the time, changes require more time than the allowed downtime. This results in creating a priority list to help with the pick order.

- **Immediate**: Produces significant loss of revenue
- **High**: Impacts a large number of users or critical users
- **Medium**: Cannot be deferred until later
- **Low**: Is needed but can wait an extended period for resolution

In any business, some periods are more critical than others. On these occasions, organizations may be frozen for changes and perform minimal operations only to avoid negative consequences, such as failure to close out books at year's end.

Cost-benefit Analysis

An alternative to the qualitative methods used earlier, quantitative methods directly measure the numbers. Though quantitative methods will present more accurate results, building and achieving the exact numbers is more challenging.

To simplify creating the analysis, it's possible to do it indirectly. Though it will be less accurate, it will be much simpler to build.

Create a list of all possible projects with both potential gains and losses (tangible and intangible). Using this information, decide which projects will generate greater business value.

It is always challenging to calculate unknown costs. Rarely is this information found in any organization. Therefore, make an educated guess by working with management to produce a weighting system that can reveal the relationship between each unknown loss and its corresponding tangible or intangible costs. Create a chart assigning ratios based on the weighting system.

Step 1: Pick one tangible known cost as the "X cost."

Step 2: Work with members of management to get their estimate (weighting system) on the related losses. The resulting table should look something like this:

Losses	Cost
Tangible Cost	
Lost user productivity	.8X
Lost IT staff productivity	.2X
Lost revenue	X
Overtime payment	.1X
Wasted goods and materials	.3X
Imposed fines	.05X
Intangible Cost	
Loss of customers	X
Loss of customer satisfaction	1.1X
Loss of business opportunity	1.3X
Damage to business reputation	1.5X
Loss of confidence in IT provider	.09X
Damage to staff morale	.9X

Table 4: Cost Ratios

In the case of tangible costs, the X is "lost revenue." The calculation from the finance team is as follows:

total annual revenue / hours per year = hourly revenue lost

(Hours per year is calculated as 365 x 24, or every hour of every day.)

Once you decide what X equals, complete the table. For this example, let's assume X = 100 US dollars.

Losses	Cost %	Total
Tangible Cost		
Lost user productivity	0.8	80
Lost IT staff productivity	0.2	20
Lost revenue	1	100
Overtime payments	0.1	10
Wasted goods and materials	0.3	30
Imposed fines	0.05	5
Intangible Cost		
Loss of customers	1	100
Loss of customer satisfaction	1.1	110
Loss of business opportunity	1.3	130
Damage to business reputation	1.5	150
Loss of confidence in IT provider	0.09	9
Damage to staff morale	0.9	90

This table allows easy comparisons and analysis.

(Overall lost revenue will not apply if the company has seasonal sales. In that case, use two rates, reflecting season and off-season sales.)

Key Performance Indicator (KPI)

Identifying KPIs to include in the plan is not an easy task. A KPI is not some nice gadget on a dashboard. Rather, it is something that management is willing to act upon. To better understand why, it is helpful to take apart the indicator:

First (indicator): Start by gathering raw data. Monitoring will generate the information. For example, volume escalated to Level II in the last week as the number of queries climbed to 100 and customers completed 50 purchases. The indicator is based on monitoring using available tools and reflects raw data.

Second (performance): Compare the indicator to the organization's capacity and capabilities to explore how it can be improved. Every indicator should include some brief language explaining how it can be decreased or increased.

Third (key): Management must decide if it wants to take any action on the indicator.

In general, there are two types of KPI: leading KPI and lagging KPI.

Leading KPI influences results, directly relating its results to the final result. An example is the number of sales visits or calls per month.

Lagging KPI measures something that has already happened. An example is the target achieved per month.

Recommendation: Don't pile on KPIs to generate an impressive dashboard. If no one is willing to act on the indicators, this becomes an unneeded effort that should be directed elsewhere.

Value Chain Analysis

Another type of analysis could be included in the plan. The term "value chain" has been used in business for years. There are three major building blocks in any value chain:

- The supplier (the source)
- The service provider (the system)
- The final customer (the outcome)

Figure 7: Value Chains

It can be tricky to calculate the value added by each action in providing service. Sometimes one weak area is offset by strength in another area. Even complementary functions may not provide added value when considered in isolation. Nevertheless, they can affect their complementary counterparts positively. Consider air-conditioning and heating. They do not create value for the business, but they do provide an environment in which workers can be comfortable and productive.

When considering the value chain, consider the entire system. Not long ago, internal business users were the only individuals to take advantage of IT. Now users are ubiquitous, turning to ATMs, web stores, points of sale, and more. Such change indicates an increasing level of value sophistication and greater expectations. Today, most businesses are expected to have an online presence reachable from virtually anywhere. Prospective customers and future revenues have become dependent on IT systems. This means you need to analyze the system's dependencies as well as other systems and functions depending on the new system.

Value Proposition Analysis

Value is realized when the return on assets is positive. Value can occur in these conditions:

- People are better utilized.
- An important resource is better managed or controlled.
- Capacity constraints can be relaxed as needed.

Most projects will relate to one of these three. Understanding how each stakeholder thinks of the value will help them absorbing the custom message. Value creation has four major parts, and each plays a role.

Customer Perception

Perception is difficult to measure because it varies from one person to another. Generally, customer perception is driven by Product or service attributes and by Preferences both are dependent on present or prior customer experiences.

Service provider value can also be influenced by a customer's perspective on cost (how much they will pay or how much it will cost the customer to do it themselves compared to the cost of an outside supplier).

Business Outcomes

Measuring business outcomes is much simpler than measuring perception. Outcomes rely mainly on customers' actual needs.

For a service to be considered valuable, it should positively impact an organization's performance or remove/relax a specific constraint.

Customers do not need services. They need fulfillment of a specific need to realize value. They don't need the printer driver; they need to print something. From an information technology (IT) perspective, printing is the service, but the customer's need is the actual printed document. The same concept applies to reports; customers don't need the reports; they need the knowledge contained in the report.

Utility and Warranty

Values depend significantly on the fit for use (utility). Can you use it for the purpose you purchase it for, and how does a warranty back up that the provider will fix it if something happens? No customer wants to have certainty in cost but uncertainty in the quality of services. Both utility and warranty are necessary to achieve value.

In some cases, a standard service utility is the same between competitors, so offering a warranty plays a more critical role and becomes a competitive advantage. Every customer would prefer good customer service, so when vendors become known for their attention to customers' needs, that often translates to a competitive edge.

Service Assets

The organization needs assets to create value. Assets can be identified as capabilities or resources.
- **Capabilities**: such qualities as likability, wisdom, employees, and management.
- **Resources**: such factors as data, application, and investment in the business. Capabilities cannot produce value without adequate resources.

Figure 8: Service Value

Business Analysis Techniques and Business Process Improvement | 35

Responsibility Matrix

Responsibility matrices are available with many variations; the most common is RACI (an acronym for responsible, accountable, consulted, and informed).

Responsibility		Explanation
Responsible	R	The one executing the action
Accountable	A	The final approval, typically, a team leader
Consulted	C	Subject matter expert
Informed	I	Keep informed
Support	S	Will provide input to the task and support the person responsible
Verifier	V	Validate the outcomes and provide QA
Out of loop	O	Not included in this task

Table 5: Responsibility Matrix Roles

To create a RACI matrix or any of its variations, use columns or rows:
- **Columns**: Build columns with headers that identify each team member or each job function.
- **Rows**: Create rows list activities, services, or whatever is necessary.

Where cells cross, fill in a responsibility. Always use people's names in the header, not job functions. This will enforce accountability. Add whatever responsibilities are necessary for the team or project. The two critical elements that must exist in every matrix are responsibility and accountability. When filling in the matrix, there can be only one accountable person per item or activity; and the person responsible must have as much support and consulting as needed. Always designate one person accountable for a given task and another person as responsible—preferably not the same person. Avoid having a single person be responsible for all actions or accountable for all actions.

	Team Member 1	Team Member 2	Team Member 3	Team Member 4	Team Member 5
Item 1	R	I	A	C	C
Item 2	A	R	S	S	I
Item 3	S	S	A	R	V
Item 4	I	R	S	A	S
Item 5	A	S	I	R	S

Table 6: RACI Matrix Example

Only fill out the cells of the contributing individuals. Otherwise, leave blank.

Role Analysis

Look at each person's column and consider the roles assigned.

- Too many As: Segregate these roles.
- Too many Rs: Consider whether one person has too much responsibility.
- No empty boxes: Consider whether it is necessary for this person to be involved in all items.

Chapter 3: From Objectives to Benefits

Any organization has two sets of activities:

- The operations
- The ability to change and enhance these operations

Business Agility

"Business agility" means the ability to respond effectively and efficiently to an operating environment and market dynamics. Changes are completed in the form of projects. One project might result in a new system or a new product. But from a business perspective, this project output is not the objective. The business objective is the outcome of this new system or product. For example, the new system will enhance productivity, and productivity will improve revenue. From a business perspective, this new product is key if it enhances productivity and improves revenue.

It is important to distinguish between decisions at each level of an organization and understand how each level has a different focus. Here is a three-tier example:

- **Operational levels**
    - Location of an order
    - The delivery date of an order
- **Tactical levels**
    - Department budget
    - Delivery performance
    - Orders to date
- **Strategic levels**
    - Annual demand for each product
    - Capacity management
    - Revenue

Project Delivery Methodology

In any project, three constraints exist:

- Scope
- Schedule
- Cost

Changing one will alter the other two. A business analyst's role is to ensure that the changes made to one constraint will impact the other two in a controlled manner.

The idea of project delivery is knowing how to get from one state to another and to manage the project as it moves from As-Is to To-Be. Two methods are available: waterfall and agile.

Waterfall Project

This project has a single-direction flow. It moves to the next step only after the current step is finished. This is the traditional way of delivering the project, and it has been around for decades.

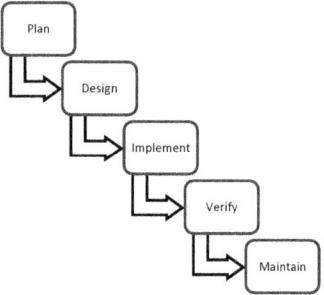

Figure 9: Waterfall Project

Agile Project

This iterative project requires envision and closing only once, but the remaining phases will go in circles until the project is finished. Sprints help produce value; the shorter, the better. The typical sprint duration is two weeks, with a maximum of four weeks. Adjust these values to fit project needs. This general terminology is adopted from the widely accepted scrum methodology.

Business Analysis Techniques and Business Process Improvement | 39

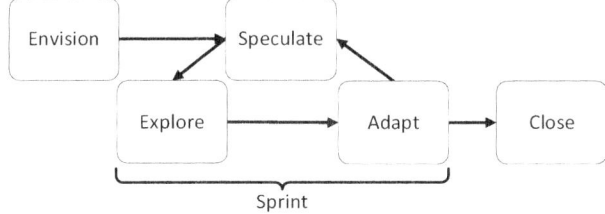

Figure 10: Agile Project

The backlog is a list of what the team has yet to deliver; it is a view of all the items in the queue.

Agile Phases

Envision phase: This phase calls for defining the project to be built, chartering the project, and building the team.

Speculate phase: This is the first phase of the sprint. This sprint requires listing features to satisfy business needs and may include delivery plan estimates and risks. Maintain a feature board showing progress and issue logs of the sprint and the overall project.

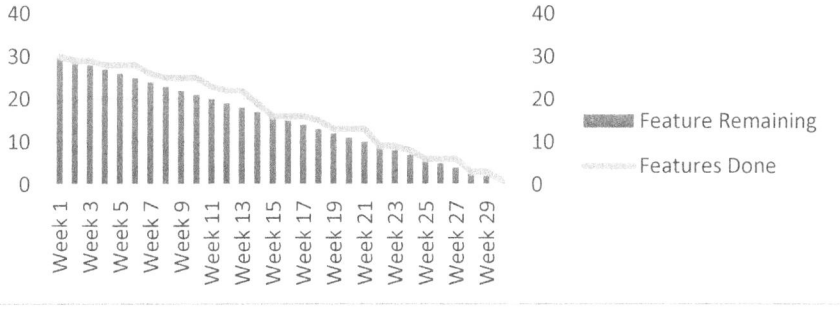

Figure 11: Backlog Chart Example

Explore phase: This is the second phase of the sprint. During this phase, the team plans the work, reviews developed features, and builds an issue management strategy. At that point, the team prioritizes the features build and estimates the time required to complete each task.

Adapt phase: This is the third phase of the sprint. It is the time to fix anything left unresolved, conduct a final review, evaluate lessons learned, collect feedback, and so on, looping through this process repeatedly until all sprints are finished.

Close phase: This final phase wraps it up, with deliverables completed and project lessons learned.

Portfolio Management

What is portfolio management? The portfolio is not a roll-up of projects and programs; it is much more than that. It is the sum of resources and assets used to achieve the business objectives and minimize risk. The portfolio is linked with organization goals, unlike the project and programs. Goals change over months and years due to dynamic marketing conditions. The organization can have one or more portfolios, but typically it will not have multiple portfolios on the same managerial level.

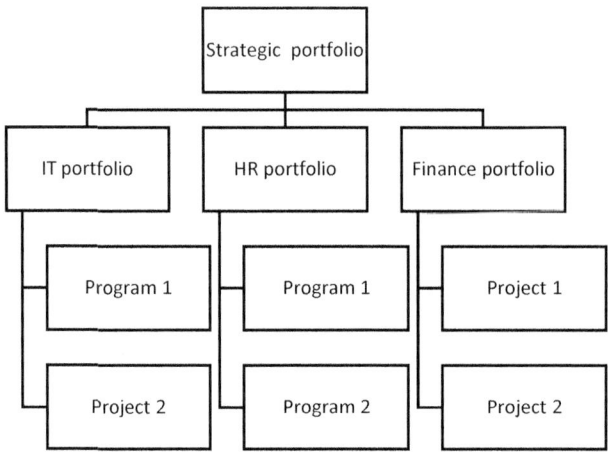

Figure 12: Portfolio Levels

The portfolio manager is not a project manager; a portfolio manager is a businessperson with some project management capabilities. His primary objective is aligning the portfolio to the business goals. In all project management methods, waterfall or agile, the methodology focuses on how to deliver the project, not the project outcome.

Business Analysis Techniques and Business Process Improvement | 41

The outcome becomes a critical factor in portfolio management that can trump decisions about costs, schedules, and resources.

The Portfolio Life Cycle

- Idea collection
- Business case and analysis
- Project feasibility
- Selection and prioritization
- Project delivery (validating outcome, not outputs)
- Benefits management

Idea Collection

There are three approaches for collecting ideas:

- Top-down
- Bottom-up
- Hybrid

Top-down Approach

Senior management creates objectives, and these goals are sent to each line of business. Each line of business, in turn, submits the objectives to its senior members and asks for project ideas.

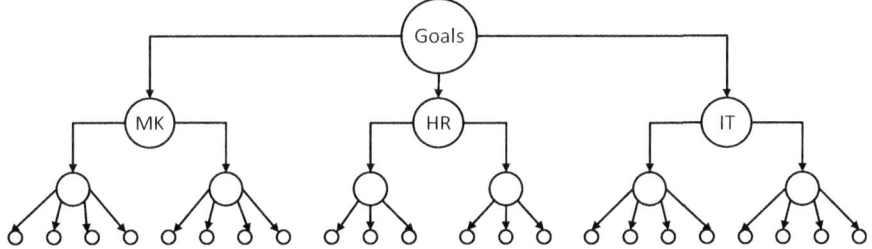

Figure 13: Top-down Approach

Bottom-up Approach

Each front-line (customer-facing) employee submits an idea, and the general organization formulates objectives based on the ideas.

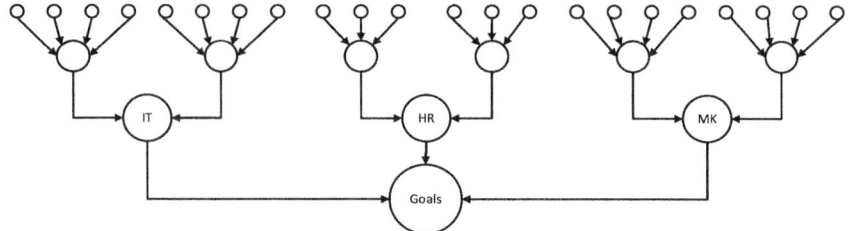

Figure 14: Bottom-up Approach

Hybrid Approach

In this approach, all organization employees, including management, contribute to the organization's final objectives and goals.

Each department's role, in this case, is to aggregate similar ideas and prioritize them according to their potential for success.

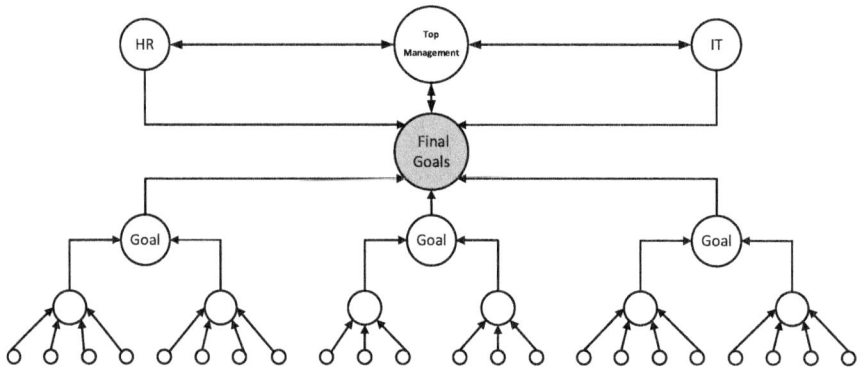

Figure 15: The Hybrid Approach

Generate Business Case

The business case demonstrates a business need (requirement) to management that justifies the investment of time, effort, and capital to achieve a specific reward. Chapter 5 is dedicated to how to build a business case.

Project Feasibility

- **Resources**: Are there enough resources (facilities, funds, time, people) available for this project?
- **Operations**: When the project goes live, can our operations team support it?
- **Capability**: Do we have experience doing it? Do we have the skills to deliver?

Project Selection and Prioritization

The selection is based on what combination of the project will deliver the organization's maximum value (internal rate of return, or IRR).

Project	Risk Budget	Cost $	IRR
Project 1	5%	100	12%
Project 2	2%	50	5%
Project 3	10%	200	20%
Project 4	1%	800	5%

Table 7: Project Selection and Prioritization

Project Delivery

Validating outcome, not output, typical project management focuses on requirements, budget, and schedule. Portfolio management focuses on benefits realized from a project. Management approves the project.

Benefits Management

Benefits management compares the benefits achieved with benefits stated in the business case and addresses any gap.

Portfolio Management Implementation

- Understand the current situation, and determine how to select and plan a project.
- Map current projects with the organization's objectives.
- Create a benefits map.
- Determine needed objectives to cover current goals.
- Prioritize projects based on matching goals to desired outcomes.
- Create a list of new projects to address unfulfilled benefits.

- Prioritize new projects based on costs and capacity.

Program Management

Program management begins with grouping two or more projects that produce similar deliverables. In other words, when it is carried out, program management has the same qualities as a project but on a much larger scale. It follows the same steps as a project. Even so, there are significant differences between a program and a project.

Why Run a Program?

The main reasons to run a program instead of several separate projects are listed below:

- Dependencies among projects inside the program
- The need to manage costs
- Coordination of activities across projects
- The need to resolve any conflicts

Program Manager Role

The program manager oversees the project managers. Therefore, the program, its projects, and its outcomes are the program manager's responsibility.

Program Life Cycle

- Program definition
- Benefits delivery
- Program closure

Program Definition

Define the program's value and benefits and start bringing projects on board. Begin this phase by adhering to the business case for the program—why it is required and the expected benefits and assumptions. The second and most crucial step in this phase is to define the program governance board. This "virtual" board consists of the sponsor and critical stakeholders. Combined, the group is responsible for the following:

- Making changes to the program projects and benefits
- Defining what the program should accomplish
- Helping keep the program on track
- Providing organizational support

Benefits Delivery

Once projects are initiated, the program design ensures that value will be delivered continuously after project closure. In this phase, create the benefits register to record and list all the planned benefits. Make sure the portfolio and register align with stakeholder needs.

Program Closure

All projects must successfully deliver the expected benefits. If not, create a delta project to close any gap.

Project Management

Project management ensures that any change to an organization's operations will positively impact or remove risk or constraint on the organization's operations.

Project Life Cycle

- **Initiation**: Create the project charter.
- **Planning**: Gather all requirements and formulate plans.
- **Execution**: Assemble the team.
- **Monitoring and controlling**: Oversee benefits to the organization, manage deliverables to maintain quality, and monitor requirements for any change.
- **Closing (project close)**: Deliver objectives and benefits to the organization.

Chapter 4: Enable the Change

A lone individual cannot accomplish this kind of project. A team is critical to success. This team will be the change agent that drives the organization to reshape and adopt the new change created by the project.

What Is a Team?

A team is a unit of two or more people who communicate and coordinate their work to achieve a specific goal.

Types of Teams

- **Formal**: created by the organization to fulfill a need
- **Vertical**: manager and subordinates
- **Horizontal**: across departments (sometimes called the project team)

Any of these types can also be defined by location:

- **Local**: a team in the same location
- **Virtual**: requiring a technology medium to facilitate communication
- **Global**: operating from different parts of the world. This team's challenge is to bridge time, distance, culture, and language.

	Formal	Vertical	Horizontal
Local Team	Team 1		Team 4
Virtual Team		Team 2	
Global Team	Team 5		

Table 8: Team Types

How to Decide on Team Size

The team should be large enough to incorporate multiple skill sets that will benefit a specific project. At the same time, it needs to be small enough to make members feel connected to one another.

Try to diversify the team. Heterogeneous teams perform better than homogeneous ones, although they will have more conflict.

Smaller teams perform faster. However, the exact number to achieve maximum success relies on many factors. Generally, from three to six members is the golden range. If more members are needed, create multiple teams, each assigned its own objectives.

Member Role

There are two main categories for members' roles; the right mix is required to reach a balance.

- **The task specialist** helps the team reach its goal.
- **The socio-emotional** member binds the team together and prevents it from falling apart.

Task Specialist	Socio-emotional
Thinks of new ideas	Supports ideas
Gives opinions	Reduces tensions (diminishes negative emotions), sometimes by telling a joke in a tense situation
Seeks information, summarizes	Harmonizes, helps solve conflicts
Energizes the team	Follows other ideas (sometimes even compromises to maintain team harmony)

Table 9: Team Members' Roles

If an entire team includes only one type of role, it will not reach its goal. For example, if the team has only task specialists, more tasks will be done; but conflicts will increase to the point that the team is no longer functional. If the team has only socio-emotional members, expect almost no conflict but slow progress.

Stages of Team Development

Any new team goes through stages to reach harmony. This is why old teams are usually much more productive than new ones.

Stage 1 (Forming)

The team is formed, and team members start getting to know each other. Situation authority typically is taken without challenge from others.

Goals are set. This stage is critical to team cohesiveness. With the correct approach, the team will agree on purpose and direction.

Team cohesiveness is a reflection of how committed members are to the team goals.

Stage 2 (Storming)

Personalities emerge; all members speak their minds and become assertive in clarifying their own roles and expectations. This will produce lots of conflicts and disagreements. In this stage, the socio-emotional role is very critical. Most teams do not get past this stage without help. They can be stuck in the storming phase unless they get help.

If conflicts in this stage are not solved correctly, the team's cohesiveness will be affected. Therefore, team leaders must be able to focus on effective conflict management and resolution. Conversely, successful conflict resolution will positively impact morale and productivity.

Stage 3 (Norming)

Once conflicts are resolved, members accept and understand one another. An informal standard starts to emerge, and that becomes the team's norm.

Stage 4 (Performing)

The focus is on team tasks and how to achieve the team goal. Disagreements are handled maturely and for the benefit of the team.

Stage 5 (Adjourning)

The team has achieved its goal and is gearing down.

I've discovered that reusing successful teams allows progress toward objectives at a much faster pace.

Effective Team Leadership

There are three main pillars of team leadership.

- **Find a purpose and rally people around it.**
  Always make sure people know the project's purpose. It is better yet if they believe in it.
- **Do not micromanage.**
  Trust the team. Members will get the job done. Even if there is some variation to the expectation, there is always more than one way to reach a goal.
- **Do not be afraid to ask for help.**
  The project leader is not expected to be an expert in all areas. It's OK to ask for help from an expert.

Conflict Resolution and Management

Conflict is when a team member tries to block the goal or ideas of another person. One of the most challenging roles of a team leader is to solve conflicts effectively. Not all conflict is bad. A mild disagreement between team members might be beneficial and prevent groupthink (going with the flow without examining contrary opinion).

The general steps for any conflict resolution are these:

1. Recognize there is a problem.
2. Accept there is an issue.
3. Express the issue.
4. Clarify and simplify points.
5. Choose how to move forward.
6. Resolve the issue.

What Is Conflict?

Conflict is opposing thoughts and feelings working against each other. These are common reasons for conflict:

- Resources
- Work style
- Perceptions
- Goals

- Pressures (often to accomplish a short-term objective)
- Roles ("It is someone else's job," or "It is my job.")
- Personal values (what's right and wrong)

One of the most common conflict sources is poor communication. A business analyst sometimes explains what the other party is communicating and makes sure the team is communicating correctly. Entire seminars are devoted to conflict resolution, where a core remedy is teaching participants how to communicate better.

Conflict in the abstract is not negative or positive. It is critical in any team. How the conflict is handled makes it positive or negative. Any conflict needs to be discussed, not avoided.

Consequences of Conflict

Here are some of the outcomes if conflicts are not addressed:

- **Miscommunication**: People will not even bother to get their points of view to the listener.
- **Quality reduction**: The team will perform at the minimum required level.
- **Missed deadlines**: The team will lack the motivation to adhere to deadlines.
- **Reduced collaboration**: Collaboration will suffer due to increased stress.

How to Handle Conflict

Behavior Types

To handle conflict, a team leader must consider the behavior types of the team members and their conflict-handling styles. That will help the team leader choose the best way to approach the problem. Behavior types generally fall into four categories:

- **Assertive**: Team members know what they want but are willing to listen and acknowledge others. (This behavior leads to win-win scenarios.)
- **Direct aggressive**: These team members seek to win at any cost. (This is either win-lose or win-win.)

- **Indirect aggressive**: People with this behavior style will try to win indirectly by blocking others from winning. (This can be win-lose or lose-lose.)
- **Passive**: People with this behavior style will not try to win and will avoid conflict at all costs. (Win-lose)

Ways to Handle Conflict

Typically, there are two approaches to handling conflict.

- **Negotiation:** searching for an agreement that satisfies both parties
- **Mediation:** aims at helping parties in disagreement listen to one another

Before starting a negotiation, first understand the goals and expectations of each person. Then plan strategy accordingly.

Conflict-handling Styles

- **Competing (Forcing) Style**: A team member seeks to compel others to accept his or her own point of view. This approach should be used only if quick, decisive action is required, usually when an urgent disaster recovery issue occurs or an unpopular decision such as layoffs needs to be made.
- **The Avoiding (Withdrawing) Style**: This may occur when an issue is trivial, or there is no chance of winning a conflict. The relationship is important.
- **The Compromising Style**: A member may use this style when both sides have equal power. The compromise may be finding a middle ground by sacrificing part of a goal and asking the other person to make a similar sacrifice.
- **The Accommodating (Smoothing) Style**: This style leads to conflict avoidance for the sake of harmony. The value of the relationship is deemed greater than the goal. This style may also be used if the accommodator is losing the conflict or is outmatched.

Business Analysis Techniques and Business Process Improvement | 53

Negotiation Outcomes

- **Win-lose**: The person who takes this approach aims to get the best possible outcome regardless of the other party's loss.
- **Lose-lose**: In this case, both sides lose something or everything.
- **Compromise**: Both parties will win, but not all needs are satisfied.
- **Win-win**: This is the best-case scenario in which both team members are happy and satisfied.

How to Reach a Win-win Solution

- Separate the people from the issue. Don't let the issue become personal or allow people to attack each other.
- Focus on interest, not demands, that is, what they want and why they need it. Seek to discern their actual interest, which may be less than what they are requesting.
- Propose multiple ways to solve the issue that might satisfy both parties.
- Set a common objective for each party and stick with it. Don't allow each party personal judgment to define what's best. A common objective will block dynamic objectives (goals that keeps shifting based on the conflict).

Organization Change

Change implementation requires considerable behavioral modification. The information in this part is intended to address the need for small changes. For major behavioral shifts within organizations, the reader will want to conduct additional research.

Organization change is the adoption of a new idea by the organization. Successful organizational change requires that the organization be poised and ready for implementation.

Before actual changes occur, the team's mission is to reduce fear and reduce negative rumors.

Usually, any organization change team includes several roles:

- **Inventor**: the team's technical member who understands the technical aspects of a solution but rarely knows how to get support for the idea
- **Champion**: the member who supports the idea, overcomes obstacles, and obtains financial and political support
- **Sponsor**: the high-level manager who protects the idea and helps remove organizational barriers
- **Critic**: the person who looks for shortcomings and ensures that ideas meet the expectation

Once the team includes all four roles, start by changing mindsets through training. The idea is to include all those who have a stake in the change (stakeholders) and educate them. This will help improve the quality of the final product (as you discover more about the need), and it will reduce fear. Remember, educate people before gathering requirements. Otherwise, there is a high risk of people dropping or hiding critical information during the interview phase.

All team members must believe in the project idea. Don't allow someone opposed to the project (or about whom you have doubts) to become a team member. Otherwise, the project will fail from the inside out.

Organization Development

Organizational culture reflects the organization's personality. Each organization has a unique culture that emerges from the beliefs and behaviors of individuals within it. It is difficult to change since it is not tangible. Rather, it is part of the chemistry of the workplace, and everyone in the organization contributes a share of it. Even so, with the correct motivation, workers can be nudged bit by bit to move in a new direction. There are three stages of changing mindsets and organizational culture: unfreezing, changing, and refreezing.

Unfreezing

All people throughout the organization are made aware of a problem and the need to fix it. This may mean describing the current state and the desired state. Always highlight the gap between current and desired performance.

Provide and update a dashboard showing both the desired target and the current status of the change. Allowing progress to be viewed fosters the unfreezing state. This dashboard should not be technical; it should be of interest to the wider business user.

For example, tracking the current incident vs. the expected incident to be solved is of interest to the support team, but not to all users. However, the productivity and financial losses due to delays in an incident may spark interest for a broader segment.

Changing

Once people become aware of the problem, introduce the new processes or technology and conduct training. Most users need to be aware of an issue to avoid resistance. Dashboard visits will indicate interest. This should be as reflected in the server administration and the server log. Taking a read count on related email notifications can be another indicator.

Refreezing

Refreezing happens when users start accepting the new system as the new normal. It is accompanied by attitude changes.

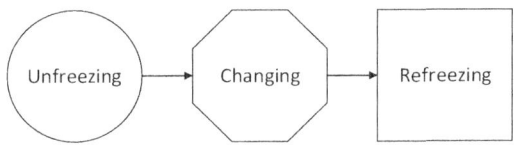

Figure 16: Unfreezing and Refreezing

Resistance to Change

The idea is to win over as many as possible within this group. In the end, there will be some who never support the project. The recommendation in such a situation is to ignore them and proceed with planned changes. Once they see the positive impact, they might change their posture.

Why Do People Resist Change?

People resist change for many reasons. These are the most common:

- **Conflict with self-interest (loss of power, prestige, benefits)**: Counter this by finding what interests each one and emphasizing its relationship to the change.
- **Lack of understanding and trust**: The employee often distrusts the reasons behind any change. Counter this with training and workshops that detail the need for change.
- **To maintain the status quo**: Some people are risk-averse or uncertain about what change might bring and therefore seek to maintain everything as is. Counter this by demonstrating the performance gap and conducting workshops.
- **Different goals**: Department managers have their own goals. Directing resources away from those goals may diminish their support for the project.

Minimizing Resistance

There are tactics to minimize the resistance to change or even overcome it:
- **Training and communication**: Don't try to hide anything. Always communicate to reduce fear.
- **Participation**: Involve workers when setting the goal.
- **Negotiations**: (See conflict resolution.)
- **The top-down approach**: Managers may compel employees to change to the new system.
- **Top management support**

Emotional Cycle of Change

If the change is significant enough, changing the way things been done for a long time, emotions might play a role. Emotions can be powerful drivers, but like other processes in business, they can transition from resistance to acceptance.

For example, let's say the improvement project is deploying a service desk tool for a ticketing system instead of the current method of dropping by or calling IT. Now the users have to follow the new system or use the new set of tools. Below are the phases for such change.

Phase 1 (Avoidance)

Customers (users) avoid the new system and repeatedly approach IT to fix issues. Here are the options to correct that behavior:
- A) Ignore any request not coming through the formal channels. This will, however, heighten the user's dissatisfaction.
- B) Fix the issue and gently ask the user to create a ticket for the change. If episodes are repeated, use the first method, apologize for taking the request this way, and cut off calling and dropping in.

Phase 2 (Performance)

Customers (users) will blame the new system for not fixing issues in time for them to perform their jobs. They will blame the service team. They will push for a return to the old system. The only solution is to continue and always show positive results. This phase will take months.

Phase 3 (Acceptance)

Customers (users) accept the new system as the new default and ask more questions on how to use it properly.

Chapter 5: Business Case

Once the project is selected, the business case should advise, inform, and convince management of what is required to address operational needs effectively. This is the most critical step. If management does not respond well to the business case, the project is canceled before it begins. Management support is essential in every upcoming aspect of the project.

What Is a Business Case?

A business case demonstrates a business need (requirement) to management that justifies investment in time, effort, and capital to achieve a given objective. The business case—half marketing and half technical—should win management support for solutions to a specific problem or requirement. It should focus on resources (people, technology, money, and time).

Here's an example:

- A recommended improvement will boost performance and increase productivity.
- The plan will allow the company to use technology better and reduce costs.
- It will increase revenue.

To gain management support for investing in your proposal, avoid statements like, "It is the right thing to do," "It makes sense," or "It's industry best practice." In other words, avoid maximizing outcomes to get a fast buy-in. If the recommendation is successful, it will be just the first of many presentations to management. But if credibility is lost in the first business case encounter, it is likely to be the last.

How Long to Build a Proper Business Case

This effort involves the work of many departments. The financial department estimates expected costs. The purchasing department reports cost estimates for needed acquisitions such as software or hardware. Finally, top management weighs in. Typically, building a business case requires 3 to 5 percent of total project time. If the plan is to finish the project in 90 days, business case preparation should not exceed one week. The more time spent on a business case, the longer the expected project duration.

How to Build a Business Case

Here are the fixed and most basic guidelines. Others can be added as needed. Stay on point. Be brief, so management can quickly read the business case. Do not exceed three pages.

The business case will be negotiable. Management may suggest other areas of focus or may wish to cut costs. In those cases, re-evaluation of the business case options may be appropriate.

Here are the basics of writing the business case:

Part 1. Executive summary: This is a paragraph explaining the purpose of the business case. Typically, this is written by a business person and placed at the beginning of the document even though it is the final piece to be written.

Part 2. Problem definition (analysis): Outline business issues. Include all issues related to quick wins so management will be eager to resolve and willing to support.

Part 3. Goals: List the desired outcomes.

Part 4. Solutions: Outline the options to solve each given problem. For each solution, define these factors:

- **Assumptions**: Assume that the project will be able to proceed as intended. For example, it can be assumed that the project will have the cooperation of the finance team to supply information on time.
- **Outcomes and benefits**: Outline the benefit of each option.
- **Cost**: Calculate or estimate the cost for each option.
- **Timeline**: Determine how long it will take to implement each option.
- **Risk assessment**: List the risks of deploying each option. Present other options that can produce differing levels of costs, risks, and outcomes.

Business Analysis Techniques and Business Process Improvement | 61

Part 5. Recommendation: Describe the best option and explain why it is recommended.

Part 6. Appendices (optional): In appendices, add financial analysis. Though this may be the most challenging part of the business case, it is helpful to demonstrate the prospective outcome with supporting data such as revenue, total cost, break-even point, fixed cost, payback period, net present value, and internal rate of return.

Draw a Fishbone Diagram

Through interviews with users, additional small issues and systems limitations will surface. These may be symptoms of a broader issue. A fishbone diagram is useful in this instance. It's a fast and straightforward problem analysis tool. The fishbone diagram is produced in three steps:

1. Draw a line.
2. Start branching out. (These will be the primary issues.)
3. Draw secondary issues that branch from the primary issues.

Upon completion, the main problem will be easily recognized along with its links to associated issues. The result will look like a fishbone. This visualization can lead to many other improvement projects and highlight the current project objective and how it contributes to solving the primary issue.

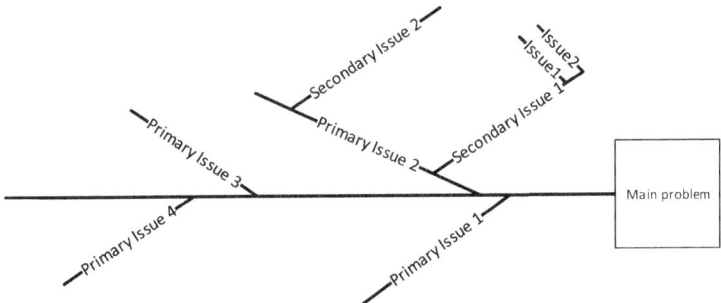

Figure 17: Fishbone Diagram

Chapter 6: Requirements and Stakeholders

After ensuring the project's feasibility and preparing the team and the organization, the next step is to inform management.

There is a high chance that not all management is involved in your project, and you might need to contact employees from departments whose managers are not involved directly. Though these managers are not directly involved, informing them is critical. This process requires talking to many decision-makers. If one decision-maker is left off the project, he or she might be offended. The bottom line for every business is people working with people. The human factor is core to success, and everyone should be treated as critical to the project. Example of a discussion opener:

"With this project, we want to improve and simplify how business is done. The effort will require the support of each department. Your contribution is crucial in developing that complete picture." Try always to think about the project and its appeal from the listener's point of view. You might find unexpected insights or champions.

During the project initiation phase, create a scope statement defining the problem, the prerequisites, and the assumptions. You will also collect requirements, identify key stakeholders, and identify the completion criteria.

Define Business Problems

Problem definition need not focus on something that is seriously wrong. A problem may indicate an interest in an issue where finding the right answers can improve an existing situation. The goal is to define business problems and potential opportunities.

- Use multiple collection techniques (individual and group interviews).
- Observe people doing their jobs.
- Review literature to avoid wasting time on previously researched topics. The literature review should include text books, internet

searches, reports, and conference materials to gain a deep understanding of the subject under consideration.
- Review the existing system.
- Collect detailed data and business perspectives on the issues from multiple sources, secondary data websites, intranet sites, annual reports, company objectives, the business plan, and operation plans. Seek primary data from knowledgeable people who are off-site.
- Find overlapping areas for improvement.

Collecting Requirements

Receive details of the project scope from the project manager and the project sponsor. Later on, in conversations with stakeholders, be alert for any areas out of scope for this project. Sometimes stakeholders will not be able to make a decision. In this case, offer alternatives to help them make a selection.

Requirements-Gathering Methods

- Interviews
- Brainstorming sessions, focus groups
- Observation of a job or a process (Get permission and give notice to the employee.)
- Surveys
- Requirements-gathering workshops: Cocreating with the stakeholders a big picture during the workshop ensures a shared understanding of the solution's vision and helps clarify the reason for the project, its goals and objectives, and its high-level scope.

A worst-case scenario occurs when, in midproject, someone discovers a requirement is missing. Sometimes it can be added. Other times, a portion of the project must be reworked, or the project must be modified.

Accurate business requirement analysis will save much rework, and there are steps to identify requirements as accurately as possible. They call for following the process of discovery, doing proper analysis, summarizing, and documenting the requirements before moving to the next stage.

Stakeholders

A stakeholder is a crucial person in the project. The individual has something to gain or lose from the project, is impacted by the work, or can influence the effort. It is essential to know the stakeholders' requirements and interests.

In some cases, all users are also stakeholders. Since it is impossible to fully engage all users, a representative sample of the user group can suffice.

The first step to identifying and knowing stakeholders is to brainstorm with the sponsor, project manager, and other key people or organizations. List the stakeholders by name, department, and organization. Avoid generic descriptions.

Internal	External
Boss	The main vendor (Jim Q. Vendor)
VP	The supplier (John M. supplier)
Users	
The technical support team	
Finance Department (John Doe)	

Table 10: Stakeholder Example

Always make sure the stakeholders clearly know the expected output from the project to avoid any potential negative impact.

Be willing to talk to as many people as time permits to explain the project, collect feedback, and identify the stakeholders. The entire project team should contribute to the list.

Identify the Project Sponsor

This might be one person or a group of people. In this case, there are two main roles:
- **The champion**: the individual who stands to benefit the most
- **The owner**: the person who will allocate the budget

In the first step, the project sponsor will do the following:

- Define the project
- Establish expectations
- Identify organizational objectives (the project's need and expected outcomes)

Identify the Target Stakeholders

How large is the stakeholder group, and where are members located? Will they request the same things or very different things?

For each stakeholder, seek your own answers to these questions:

- What do they value in this project?
- Do they support or oppose project objectives?
- What are their levels of commitment?
- Do they have the authority to change outcomes?
- Did we collect their requirements?
- What areas of the project might be a conflict for which stakeholders?

Identify Business Requirements

Collect the needed requirements from designated stakeholders. Eliciting requirements is as simple as asking the right questions.

Each stakeholder may consider the project from a unique perspective, and each may identify requirements far beyond the project scope. Managing expectations is critical in this stage.

Analyzing the requirements means understanding answers and recognizing related questions that can complete the concept of each idea and how its pieces connect.

Collection Techniques

Interviews and focus groups are the two main collection techniques.

Interviews: Talk to each stakeholder. A guided interview is preferable. Create just a few simple questions in advance to guide the interview properly.

Focus groups: Group members provide input while showing the integration points between departments.

In rare cases, a previous attempt at this specific improvement might exist. Reviewing the previous documentation or discussion with involved people might be helpful.

Types of Pain

Pain is a term used to describe an issue or a problem from the business perspective. Mainly there are three types:

- **Latent pain**: This type of problem has existed for so long in the customer realm that the company lives with it day to day or has found a way to work around it.
- **Current pain**: A customer recently discovered the problem and is asking for help in finding a solution.
- **Possible pain**: This is a problem already recognized that will present problems for customers in the future unless action is taken.

All business challenges boil down to three simple goals:

- Revenue increase
- Cost decrease
- Risk management

The business analyst needs to recognize which requirements fall within these categories. Never assume you know specific answers to the questions. Always ask, even if the answers seem obvious.

Prepare for the Meeting

Before each meeting, the business analyst should create an agenda. It must contain the purpose of the meeting, the expected outcome, and the topics to be discussed.

Interviews

Learn the needs from each interviewee's point of view. Meet when stakeholders are available. Typically, start at a management level to learn core requirements; and focus on frontline levels to observe how the company conducts business. For most users, a single interview is enough, but be prepared in some cases to conduct a follow-up interview for needed clarifications. The primary objectives of the interviews are these:

- To gather information
- To understand needs
- To build a positive relationship and gain trust
- To have the interviewee's opinion without peer pressure

As much as possible, make the interview a two-way conversation and approach it with a positive attitude. If it is a one-way session in which you ask all the questions, it will become counterproductive and feel to the interviewee like an interrogation.

Be prepared to tailor interviews to all types of stakeholders:

Sponsor interview: Expect to learn about the project from a business perspective in this interview. The focus of the interview should be on the current issue and the business goals.

Function leader: This person will explain the project from only their point of view.

End user: This interviewee can talk about the system, the process limitations, and inconsistencies.

Prepare for the Interview

Most stakeholders have jobs to do, so be prepared, where possible, with basic background knowledge of the challenges interviewees face. Keep interviews as short as possible.

Begin by defining a topic for the interview and drafting a meeting agenda. Get the interviewee manager's necessary approvals.

Set the first interview with the project sponsor and ask for recommendations of other key stakeholders to interview. Ask these people, in turn, to suggest others who should be interviewed.

Work with the project manager to determine the list of stakeholders. This is critical. Sometimes the lists provided are best guesses, and not all individuals identified will have needed

Business Analysis Techniques and Business Process Improvement | 69

information. Therefore, when a name is offered, ask why the person is recommended and what knowledge they can share.

Prepare the Questions

When planning the interview, prepare two types of questions:

- **Open-ended:** Descriptions, what, how, and so on
- **Closed-ended:** Basic questions that can be answered simply or with "yes" or "no" responses.

Always start with an open-ended question. Validate or clarify the answers with closed-ended questions.

Not all stakeholders are equal. It helps to know their roles in the project and their impact.

Sometimes the interviewee may have no information to share. In this case, end the meeting graciously to maintain the relationship.

Conducting the Interview

Make sure you understand the big picture from the stakeholders' points of view. Otherwise, you risk missing essential requirements or key elements of their knowledge.

Start by preparing questions to ensure you are talking to a knowledgeable person who can contribute to the requirements. Typically, group the questions into four areas:

- What is your vision for this project?
- What is the current situation?
- What is considered a success for the project?
- What are the risks of this project?

To build rapport, you must understand the interviewee. A project you previously worked on together, personal interests outside of work, or other areas of common ground may aid rapport. If you have no previous connections, seek rapport in the discussion about the current project, what it will achieve, and its importance.

Set expectations. Sometimes a person is unaware of the project. Be prepared to give a briefing about the goals, vision, and stakeholders' needs. (A typical interview can be 30 to 60 minutes.)

Cultivate information flow from the interviewee. Do not phrase questions in a way that loads them with information or assumptions. Instead, let the interviewee give all possible information. Don't stray into technical requirements. These typically will come when you design the solution. The focus here is the business value, not the technical value. Focus too on problems or challenges, not solutions, during these sessions.

Follow up on the interview

Always send a post-interview email thanking the interviewee for spending time and sharing ideas with you.

Send the interviewee a detailed overview of what was discussed. This becomes both a helpful record of what you learned and an opportunity to check for accuracy in your understanding and interpretation of the points made. Encourage the stakeholder to respond further if there was any misunderstanding. Include any decisions made and review any next steps.

Categorize Stakeholders

Two factors determine the stakeholder level—how much power and influence the person has over the project, and the person's level of support for, or opposition to, the project.

Place each stakeholder into a group based on the level of influence and interest. Members can be positive and want the project to succeed, or they can be negative and want it to fail.

The negative impact may be caused by an emotional response to the project's goals or even to a change in the status quo.

Typically, there are four primary stakeholder groups:

- **Keep Informed**: These people have low influence and low interest in the project. Usually, a clear majority of users are in this group.

Business Analysis Techniques and Business Process Improvement | 71

- **Consult**: This group includes anyone who can provide input that can benefit the project, either by voicing positive ideas or offering constructive criticism. These members are interested but have minimal influence (usually peers and interested users).
- **Involve**: This group is crucial because members have influence but low interest in the project. The objective is to involve them and learn which of their interests may be achieved in the project. The aim is to provide any project-related information they may need to become involved.
- **Main players**: These are the most crucial stakeholders. The key is to communicate carefully with these members to maintain their positive interests. For those in this group who feel negatively, explore what knowledge of the product might bring a positive response.

Map of the Key Stakeholders

Since not all stakeholders possess the same levels of influence or interest, a stakeholder map can help visualize the groups.

Start with a square divided into quadrants 1, 2, 3, and 4. Subdivide each of those quadrants into A, B, C, and D. Use the figure to easily chart members on a spectrum as follows:

- A: High influence of the group, less interest than group B
- B: High influence, highest interest
- C: Low influence, lower interest than group D
- D: Low influence but highest interest

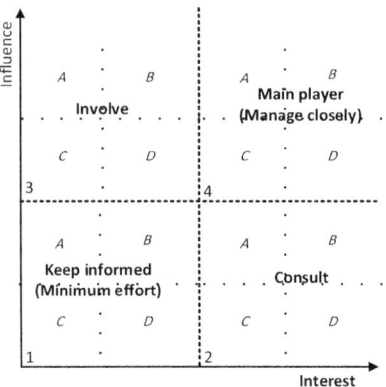

Figure 18: Stakeholder Map

From the above, build a table to identify the stakeholders.

Stakeholder	Quadrant	Subgroup	Interest
Boss	4	B	Positive
VP	4	A	Positive
Users	1	B	Positive
Technical support team	2	D	Positive
Finance Department (John Doe)	3	A	Negative
Main vendor (Jim Q. Vendor)	1	D	Positive
Supplier (John M. Supplier)	2	A	Negative

Table 11: Stakeholder Table Map Example

Communication Plan

A communication plan is a guide for how to provide the right messages to the right people at the right time. Usually, the communication effort is for key stakeholders. A typical communication plan contains the following:

- Stakeholder name
- Title
- Project role
- Key interest and issues
- Preferred communication approach (email, phone, in person, etc.)
- Messages needed (presentations, project updates)
- Frequency of messages

Business Analysis Techniques and Business Process Improvement | 73

- Communication channels (email, phone numbers, etc.)
- The person responsible for sending communications

Stakeholder names	Title	Project role	Key interest and issues	Communication approach	Massages needed	Frequency	Channel	Delivered by
Mr. John	Marketing executive	Consultant	duration of the project	Email	presentation	monthly	in person	Team leader
Mr. Doe	Senior financial analyst	Consultant	cost of the project	Phone	presentation	weekly	phone	Project manager

Table 12: Communication Plan Example

Both of these tables are dynamic. They are not built once and forgotten. People do change their interests. Watch for changes and update each table as appropriate.

Categorize Features

Categorizing features is similar to placing a tag on the feature. The primary reason for the categorization is how the features are developed.

Categorize the Types

Once all requirements are collected from all stakeholders, begin categorizing them into the following groups:

Functional refers to what a solution should do. For example, the solution should improve response time to orders to less than 5 seconds.

Nonfunctional describes the situation and environment in which the solution operates. For example, the uptime for a solution is 99.99 percent of the time.

Technical requirements are related to how the system is built. For example, it may detail a given configuration for a specified operating system.

Transition requirements may serve as a temporary bridge to installing improved operating systems. An example is when old data is migrated into a new system capable of more sophisticated functions.

The Importance of Features

After the core information is collected, evaluate why the feature is needed. Is it a must? A should? Or nice to have?

Ensure that the collected requirements reflect current business strategies. Always ask stakeholders to categorize requirements by importance.

A **"must" feature** is core to the business, which depends on it.

A **"should" feature** is a core feature that will speed the software cycle (such as simple reporting functionality).

A feature that is nice to have is aimed at user comfort and ease of access.

If a stakeholder does not know how to prioritize requirements, use MoSCoW method (M - Must have S - Should have C - Could have W - Won't have). Apply the model to every possible requirement, and assume that none can be delivered. The impact of not doing the requirement will help determine if it is "must have," "should have," "nice to have," or "will not have."

Requirements Traceability Matrix (RTM)

The objective of the RTM is to track who asked for what feature.

Reference	Requirement	Importance	Type	Stakeholder
REQ01	Uptime 99%	Must	Nonfunctional	Jane
REQ02	Simple process for the order	Should	Functional	Jon

Table 13: Requirements Traceability Matrix Example

This matrix is easily expanded to add (and track) more requirements. The RTM's primary objective is to track the requirements' progress from the initial collection until its delivery. Depending on the project size, you could have one matrix or multiple. However, it's best to start with a spreadsheet and keep adding columns when needed, such as the requirement acceptance status, the verification status, and so on. When adding something, increase the version number of the matrix and expand it to fit the need. Things you might include:

Business drivers (like why we do this, what needs to be included, and how we will do that)

Project Drivers (project objectives, project deliverable, use case)

Delivery (test case number, verified by acceptance criteria, status)

Requirement Refinement and Verification

After completing the RTM, the next step is to ensure all the requirements are quality and accepted.

Requirement Quality Checklist

Explore whether the requirement meets the following criteria:

- Necessary
- In-scope
- Specific
- Measurable
- Achievable

For each requirement, ask these questions:

- Who/what is most impacted by this project (for example, people, the organization, equipment)?
- What was the original scope of the system?
- Where is it (local, remote, in multiple cities or countries)?
- When did this need first appear?
- How many customers and users are impacted?
- Which location faces the most challenging issues?
- Why is the project needed?

Verification

Peer Review: Find someone who is not a stakeholder to identify any vague areas or words. You have other project managers, users, customers, and sponsors unrelated to your project who can bridge the gap to ensure everyone's understanding of the requirements is the same.

Formal Review: A legal team needs to review the requirements word by word.

Always validate the requirements against the rules enforced by the business. A business rule, for example, might establish a maximum number of times a bank customer may make ATM withdrawals in a single day.

Acceptance Criteria

Acceptance criteria are the deliverables of high-level business requirements. The requirements must be measurable and clear.

Testing

Build a test plan document that describes what and how the requirement will be tested, by whom, and when. The plan includes the following:

- Scope and objectives
- Testing roles
- Tools and documents
- Entry and exit criteria

This is a high-level document created to group similar requirements to test them in a batch and define who will test them. At this point, you are required only to define the high-level items mentioned. Later, this will be expanded to create test cases that map to the requirements.

Managing Customer Expectations

This measure has a simple focus: Does the project or service meet customer expectations? Or does it fall short?

Typically, expectations are derived from the following:

- Communications
- Similar past experiences
- Word of mouth
- Other projects in use

Conduct a workshop with stakeholders to verify all gathered requirements and address any requirements that were dropped and why. There are many reasons a requirement must be abandoned or transformed. To avoid surprises, communication is imperative. Here are the steps:

1. Contact the stakeholder in question.
2. Explain why a requirement must be eliminated. For example, it will take too long to implement, be in the next phase, or be too expensive.
3. Offer a list of alternatives. Maybe a requirement from another stakeholder will satisfy the need.
4. Agree on a solution. (The stakeholder might rephrase the request to be compatible with another requirement or ensure that it is funded.)

Build a Requirements Package

The final step is to build a requirements package. This is where all the documents created so far will be linked to present the final accepted package to the project team to act on.

The project charter describing the expected improvements is the first item in your requirements package.

The requirements document should incorporate the following sections:

- Who provided requirement data, and what was required
- Constraints of the requirement
- Assumptions
- Dependencies

Decision Tables

Sometimes you might be faced with a functional requirement that presents many solutions. It's easier to document such complex requirements in a decision table explaining the rules and how the system should react based on the input. Usually, this part is considered part of the design of the system.

When you have many factors that will guide a decision, place them in a decision table. This will identify all possible scenarios. For greatest efficiency, use these limitations:
- Use only yes-no questions (not values).
- Limit the table to four or five factors. Need more? Make a new table. That's because adding a single column can significantly increase the number of scenarios. In short, the more columns, the more possible outcomes (5^5 = 25 scenarios, 4^4 = 16 scenarios, 3^3 = 9 scenarios).

	from 1 to 50 units	1000+ units?	Is it a local city?	Decision
1	Yes	No	No	Yes
2	No	Yes	No	No
3	No	No	Yes	No
4	Yes	Yes	No	Yes
5	No	Yes	Yes	No
7	Yes	No	Yes	Yes
8	Yes	Yes	Yes	Yes
9	No	No	No	No

Table 14: Decision Table Example

Collecting Requirements in Agile Teams

"Agile" is an umbrella term for a group of methodologies, so the produced document changes depending on which methodology is used. But these are the highlights.

The documentation in an agile team is lightweight and straightforward. As you see from the agile phases depicted in Figure 19, the focus is on producing results for the business. Compared with the waterfall method, this may require many more hours to document requirements. In agile, the approach is to spark conversation to deliver value.

Continuous alteration in agile allows for refinement of the requirement with each release. Stakeholders can redefine requirements as needed.

For backlog items or features, the business analyst will prioritize the essential features in the next or future releases. The business analyst and the owner will ensure most of the backlog will be removed during the refinement process, eliminating work that will not provide value.

Business Analysis Techniques and Business Process Improvement | 79

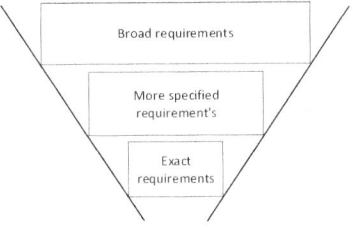

Figure 19: Requirements in Agile

The primary objective is to keep the agile sprints going on. Focus on estimating, analyzing, prioritizing, and breaking down stories for each next sprint. Several meeting workshops and sessions will be conducted to refine each upcoming sprint and to address the backlog. Here's how:

Split the user story: The business analyst will divide the user story into smaller pieces that are not technical functions. Instead, these pieces represent customer value that can be presented, quantified, and tested.

Build a story map: Tackle each user story in the logical order for the process. This means producing a grid that may look like this:

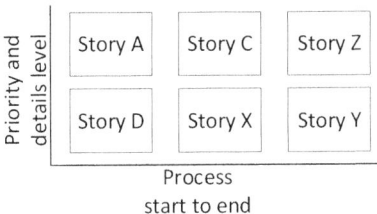

Figure 20: Story Map

Chapter 7: Business Process Modeling

The real challenge in any process is starting where you are and introducing further development. The start point is the process road map. The proposed model has five main areas:

- Documenting the current situation (process modeling and mapping)
- Normalizing and improving the process
- Optimizing the process by statistical means
- Automating the process (two levels)
- Implementing full automation and real-time optimization using AI/ML

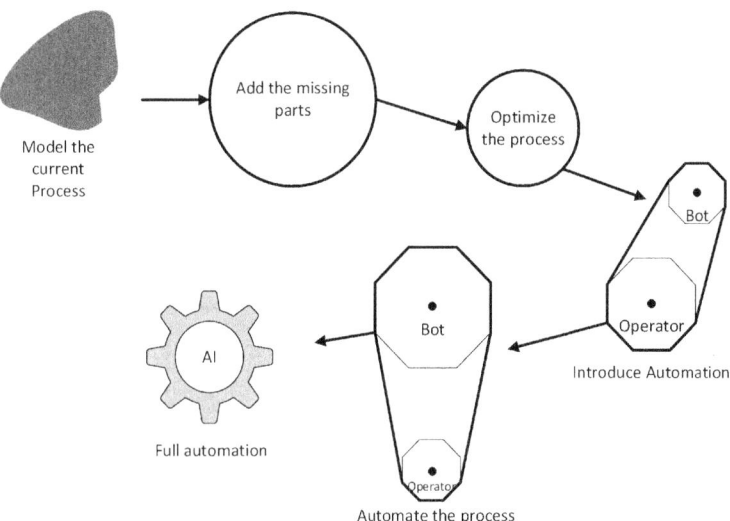

Figure 21: Process Evolution

Each phase is not an upgrade; it's an entirely different format that the business may or may not need. For example, if you are building a software system and all you need is to model the process for that system, it's perfectly OK to stop after the process modeling.

Understanding the Process

Any business relies on a set of processes (systems) connected to deliver value to an end customer. Documenting these processes is critical for an organization to stay competitive.

Business process modeling (BPM) is a visual way for an organization to keep track of its processes and ensure that they are in alignment with goals and objectives.

The main benefit of BPM is understanding how an organization runs and performs its activities. This effort can help identify vague or missing processes within the organization.

Start by identifying the steps included in BPM. The following tools are most commonly used with the model:

- Context diagram (high-level understanding of interactions)
- Functional flow diagram (the process between actors)
- Swimlane diagram (the process across all involved entities)
- Flowcharting (the process geared to someone specifically)

Next, build the As-Is model. The As-Is documents the current situation in the organization, with no improvements or adjustments. Chances are that organizations adapting such projects are operating and have some system in place to perform this function. The organization has likely established some processes to provide users with services.

If you are in the rare situation of starting the process from scratch, follow the same steps as the users wish and inject the application design on top of it, adding things like login screens, and save work.

What Is a Process?

A process is a transformation action toward one or more goals. It's measurable, has a specific result, and has a particular trigger. This definition is very general and can be applied to almost anything. The closest analogy is the conveyer belt, which starts and ends in a specific location and can carry a specific set of items (such as boxes with a set minimum and maximum size). You could link multiple belts to make an assembly line that starts out with components and ends up with the finished product.

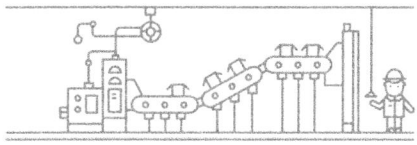

Figure 22: Factory

This is precisely is a business process. However, it's a bit smarter than that. Based on your input, it can redirect you to another process and place logic inside it.

What Is Organizational Capability?

An organization can achieve a specific company-wide benefit through multiple specialized processes. It is not limited to IT. Capacity management, for example, is an organizational capability, not a process. Capabilities usually involve experience-driven and knowledge-intensive resources such as financial capital, infrastructure, and the ability to implement. It is easier to obtain resources than to acquire capabilities.

Capabilities develop over time through the experience of solving problems, finding solutions, dealing with risk, and analyzing failures.

Let's take a more straightforward example. The organization is a car driving in a city, which represents the market. Navigating the city without asking for directions (or setting a point on the GPS) is a capability. Finding shortcuts, avoiding traffic jams, and getting to your destination are good capabilities. As with driving, not every direction the GPS gives you is good, and not every shortcut is in the GPS. Being lost and trying out different directions give you experience. And the same is true for the capability.

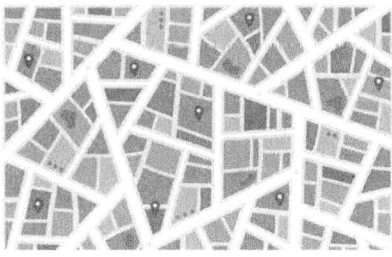

Another example is that order fulfillment is an excellent capability at Amazon, as user experience is for Apple.

Discover and Draw the Current Services

Before contemplating any improvement in existing processes, it is crucial to know the organization's current setup status. Any spontaneous move to enforce a process or develop a capability that conflicts with the existing business will result in project failure.

The idea behind all of these BPM diagrams is to have a reference point that will focus on what is needed. Typically, hundreds of processes exist in any given organization. Upgrading or modifying any components requires knowledge of the data used and the person who deals with it. Otherwise, you risk impacting other processes or creating a zombie process that takes up resources but does not generate value. Therefore, a deeper and more informed understanding of the entity, its activities, and its data flow is required before any change.

How to Document a Current System

There is a high chance that the organization's department documentation is outdated. How does one document an existing system?

Any request for help likely will arrive as a business operations matter, not a technical request. Furthermore, it is critical to first understand and document the business side of the issue and, afterward, translate the need on the technical side.

The process of documenting the existing processes has three main steps:

1. Conduct interviews and create an activity list.

2. Build data flow diagrams.
3. Build flowcharts and swimlanes.

To make this fast, plan the first half of the day as a one-hour one-on-one interview with the owner and a two-hour session with a group of users who use this process daily to build the process branches. Use the remainder of the day to create the list, the process, and the flow diagrams. This setup allows getting back to the users for questions on the same day.

Create an Activities List

The first step is to build a responsibility matrix by asking the owner how the existing process and its variations function. (If no owner is available, turn to the frequent users.)

This becomes a what-if scenario: Create a new table whenever a new branch starts for a new activity. Document the narrative and start building the activity table. (See Table 15.)

Don't use a recorder; it makes many people uncomfortable. Instead, take notes and confirm general understanding.

Any activity requires an entity or an action to trigger it. Typically, this will be a person or a problem.

Let's take building a support request as an example. Sit down with a support representative to ask about the process of printers, for example. Here is what you might learn:

*In IT support, many cases are related to **printers**. In some cases, we need to start an order for a new printer. In another case, it's just the driver installed on the system. Sometimes it may be a minor issue in the printer that can be easily fixed by the **user**, like a paper jam. Other cases require IT, or **toner** replacement, or a return to the **manufacturer** for maintenance.*

*Boldface words are entities in our activity.

Start with IT's first scenario to get a new printer for the user. This is the first branch. Get details on the process followed to make an acquisition. Get details for the steps involved.

The user contacts IT by phone or email to request a printer. The request is sent to the user's manager via email for approval. Then the approval is sent to the purchasing department for the printer acquisition. The supplier delivers the printer. IT engineers collect it from the warehouse and move it to the end-user location. Users grant us access to work on their laptops. We install and make the necessary configurations. Once done, the user tests the printer and provides us with the sign-off.

* This overview represents the IT point of view.

From the detailed description above, we can extract an activity list. In the table, data processing is marked in bold, and external entities are underlined.

Entities	Activities
User	1. Contact IT support.
IT support	2. Pick up the phone/read email.
	3. Read/listen to the requests.
	4. **Write request approval for the user's manager.**
Manager	5. **Approve/Reject**
IT	6. Send the approval to the purchasing department.
	OR
	Notify the user of rejection.
Purchasing	7. Send a request to the supplier.
Supplier	8. Deliver the printer.
Warehouse	9. Receive the printer.
	10. **Notify IT via email.**
IT helpdesk	11. Collect the printer from the warehouse.
	12. **Update the record with supplier warranty.**
	13. Deliver the printer to the user location.
User	14. **Grant access to the machine**
IT helpdesk	15. Install the printer.
	16. **Make the necessary configurations.**
User	17. **Test the printer.**
	18. **Provide sign-off.**
IT Helpdesk	19. **File the sign-off.**

Table 15: Activities List Example

Using the list in Table 15, describe the entities: Are they internal (controlled by IT) or external (IT cannot control)? Describe the activities: Do they involve data processing, i.e., do they change the state of information? Or is data merely moved?

Shape Meanings

Primary shapes are used in the following diagrams:

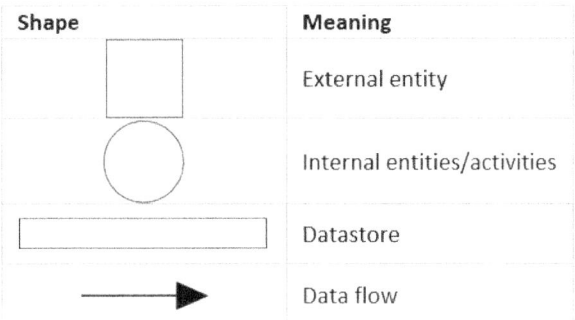

Shape	Meaning
▢	External entity
◯	Internal entities/activities
▭	Datastore
→	Data flow

Table 16: Diagram Shapes

Context Diagram

This diagram provides a high-level, at-a-glance view of internal and external entities. The internal entity is the organization. The external entities can be suppliers and banks; or a department, team, system, or process within the organization that interacts with external entities. This might be characterized as an us-or-them diagram. The external entities are not the focus of the context diagram. Each arrow represents a process or subprocess.

The main reason for creating a context diagram is to understand the interaction between the primary entity (the system in our example) and the interactions and dependencies with other systems. Later, it will point to other processes in the system that need further documentation.

Drawing a context diagram is fairly simple. Start by drawing the first context diagram with the organization and external entities.

In each relationship, find the internal entity and draw a new context diagram. Keep doing this until all relevant entities have context diagrams.

The context diagram is meant to define system boundaries. It is a logical, abstract diagram. To build a context diagram, follow three steps:

- **Step 1:** Start by writing the process name being documented. (This shape will link to all the internal entities.)
- **Step 2:** Write the names of all external entities, each one in a separate box.
- **Step 3:** Add arrows, each with an abstract activity (nouns only). Summarize multiple processes in a single arrow.

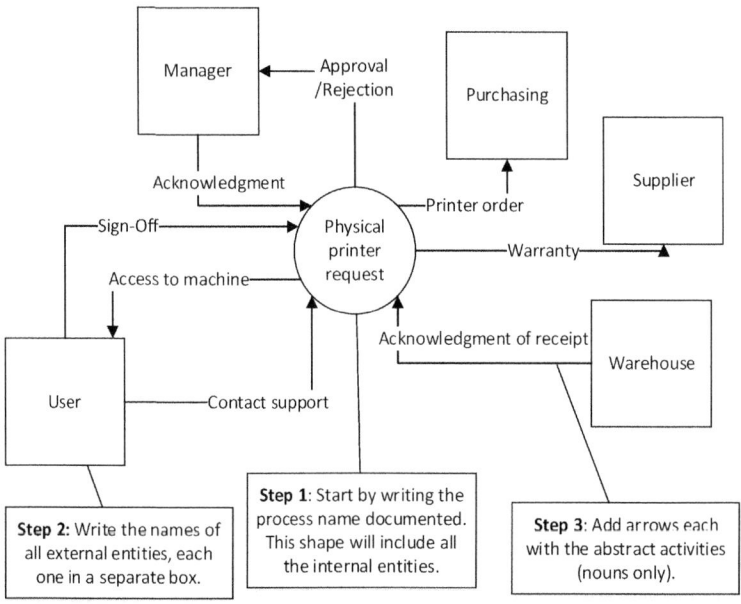

Figure 23: Context Diagram Example

Physical Data Flow Diagram (PDFD)

The PDFD follows the exact steps cited in the activities list. A simple approach is to take the context diagram, remove the text from the internal entities (circles), and replace it with internal activities. The diagram should follow the top-down activities list data flow to avoid confusion. Instead of having a single circle with a physical printer request, the PDFD will have three (email system, IT support, and record system).

The PDFD is more concerned about the system used to get the final result delivered. This is how the system is implemented, in other words. If you are building software, each internal component of the PDFD will have at least one screen dedicated to it, and each external component will mean an integration point.

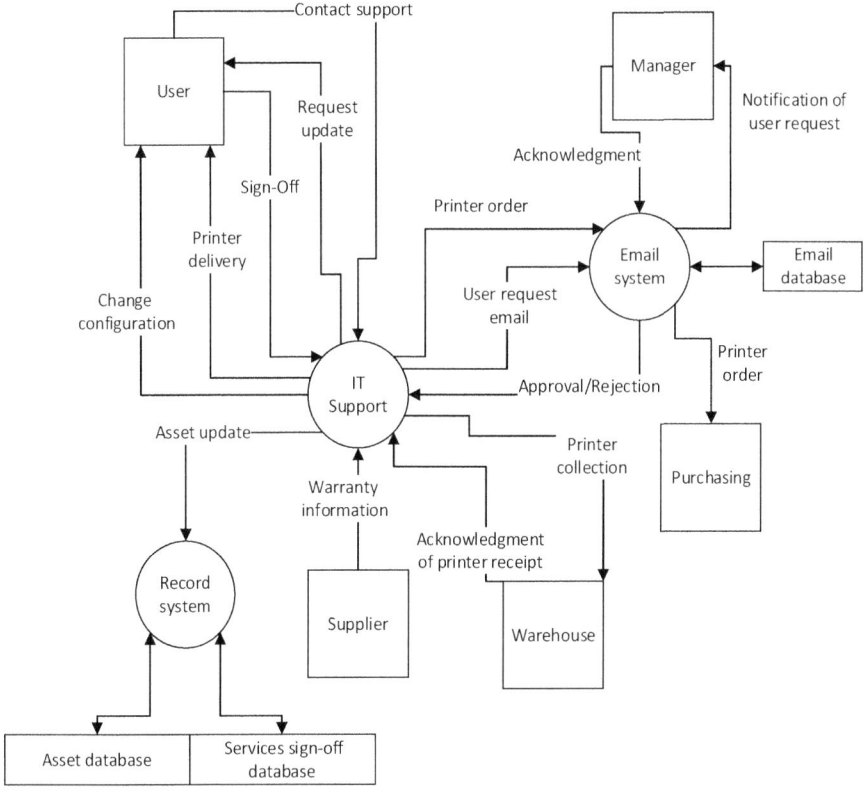

Figure 24: PDFD Example

Logical Data Flow Diagram (LDFD)

The primary reason for building an LDFD is to extract the process and the system's business rules as well as where the data should be coming from and where it should be stored. The result of LDFD is to understand the inputs/outputs of the system. Typically, most of the LDFD is hidden from an end user.

A conceptual diagram focuses on the activities and who is doing them. In this diagram, group activities are based on location and execution order.

Entities		Activities	Group	Group Name
User	1.	Contact IT support	A	Receive request
IT support	2.	Pick up the phone/read the email	A	
	3.	Read/listen to the request	A	
	4.	Write request approval from the user's manager	A	
Manager	5.	Managers approve/reject	B	Approve workflow
IT	6.	Send the approval to purchasing OR Notify the user of rejection	B	
Purchasing	7.	Send a request to the supplier	C	Acquire printer
Supplier	8.	Deliver the printer	C	
Warehouse	9.	Receive the printer	D	Deliver printer
	10.	Notify IT via email	D	
IT helpdesk	11.	Collect the printer from the warehouse	E	Install printer
	12.	Update the record with supplier warranty	E	
	13.	Deliver the printer to the user location	E	
User	14.	Grant access to the machine	E	
IT helpdesk	15.	Install the printer	E	
	16.	Make the necessary configurations	E	
User	17.	Test the printer	E	
	18.	Provide sign-off	E	
IT helpdesk	19.	File sign-off	E	

Table 17: LDFD Groups

Now, label A, B, C, D, E, groups by the order in which they are executed. Next, start from the context diagram to make the connections. Use the table as a guide to link each lettered group with its circle.

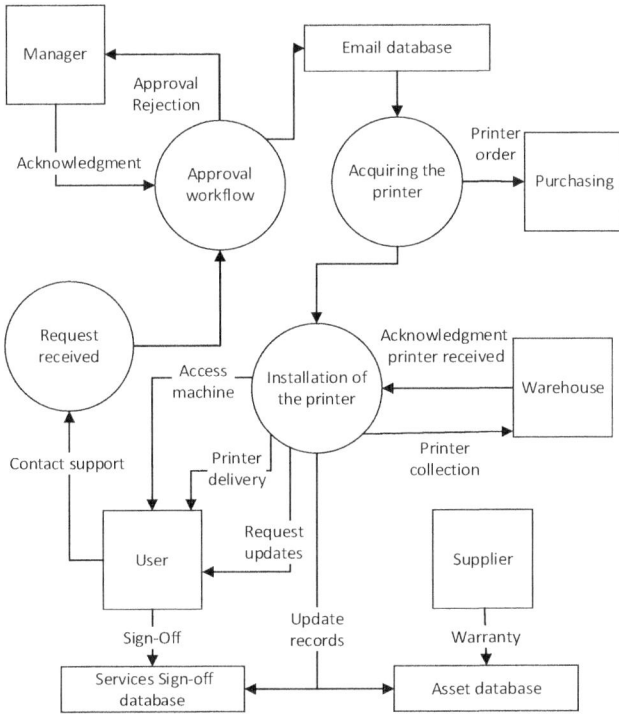

Figure 25: LDFD

Usually, both PDFDs and LDFDs are used in the initial high-level stage. Later on, include more technical diagrams like ERD and UML.

Drawing a Flowchart

Before we begin, here's a brief definition of flowcharts and how they work.

What Is a Flowchart?

The flowchart is a representation of the start and end of a process that follows a logical order. It gives a picture of steps necessary to achieve a specific purpose.

Flowchart Symbols

The table below shows the primary symbols used for flowcharts.

Symbol	Meaning
(rounded rectangle)	**Start/end of chart:** This symbol is the first and last symbol in any flowchart. It starts and finishes the entire flow. Example: A call received from an end user can be a start Or An incident solved can be the end.
(diamond)	**Decision:** This is a yes/no or true/false query. This question and answer can focus on any topic but will be reduced to true-or-false logic. This ensures that all decisions can be simplified. Example: Did the previous steps solve the user problem? Yes. It will lead to the end path. Or No. It will direct to a different path.
(rectangle)	**Process/Action:** This process usually is used to receive input from another shape. It can be adding, subtracting, dividing, creating, or building. Example: Building the activities list or Subtracting the cost from the customer account
(arrow)	**Arrow:** This represents the connection direction between any two shapes. Usually, this is top-down.
(document shape)	**A document (paper)**
(cylinder)	**A database or file on the computer:** Used to store or retrieve data
(parallelogram)	**Output data:** Used after some activities that produce data
(trapezoid)	**Manual Actions:** For example, calling someone or writing something down
(subprocess shape)	**Subprocess:** a branching process
(circle / pentagon)	**On-page/off-page connector:** Arrows may go in all directions when drawing a complicated process. This helps clean things up a bit. A circle for on-page refers to an item on the same page. (It usually has a number in it to identify the linkage.) The second shape refers to an item off-page if the chart spans multiple pages. (It also contains a number to identify the intended off-page link.)

Table 18: Flowchart Symbols

Building a Flowchart

Linear, swimlane, or cross-functional charts are a variation of the same concept. Depending on how many actors, parties, or functions are involved, the name changes, but all types are generally called "flowcharts."

Business Analysis Techniques and Business Process Improvement | 93

There is a simple process I like to perform before I use the drawing tools to create the final flowcharts:

1. Get a flipchart, cut down the pages, and stick them on the wall. Consider each one a process page.
2. On sticky notes, write down activities and arrows. Ask available volunteers to move the sticky notes to the correct places. If you use an on-screen drawing tool instead, people will look for the shortest path because making changes with the drawing tool requires much more effort than moving a sticky note.
3. Keep the flow as simple as possible. (Ask yourself if a 10-year-old can understand the flow. If not, simplify.)
4. Keep the details consistent throughout the entire map.
5. There should be no loops. If a problem is not fixed, don't start over and repeat work unnecessarily. Each action should involve several possible solutions. Alternatively, try to transfer the issue to a more specialized process. To avoid loops, add a decision with a count. (How many times a ticket ID was received, for example.)
6. Try to keep the flow in one direction, top-down or left-right. Don't point arrows in all directions. That adds confusion. (Remember, a 10-year-old needs to understand it.)
7. Add any shape, but include a diagram key to identify which shapes represent what.

Once all team members agree on a valid process, proceed with the actual flowchart using drawing tools.

Drawing Swimlane Charts

As a rule, if the entire process is performed by a single actor (entity), use traditional top-down flowcharts. If there are many actors, use a swimlane chart. Likewise, if the process is complicated and has many steps, use swimlane to demonstrate the interactions between actors. For each actor, use a flowchart. Since our example is simple, we will use a swimlane to cover all activities.

The swimlane flowchart is a repository for data from multiple flowcharts. It is based on internal and external entities from the

PDFD and the connections from the LDFD. Entities can be vertical or horizontal, although vertical is easier to read.

Typically, a swimlane chart is a high level with lots of subprocesses. Each subprocess has its own flowchart.

If you find this overwhelming, I would advise you to start with a high level and then drill deeper whenever needed.

- **Level 1 process:** Level 1 is called the block-based process and is relatively easy to do because you can demonstrate the process at the first level in just a few steps. Level 1 is typically when you want to confirm the understanding *or* when you don't have enough time to build a complete process.
- **Level 2:** Take each block and break it down into more clear steps.
- **Level 3:** Take a block from Level 2 and break it down further.

Continue doing so until you reach the desired level of detail.

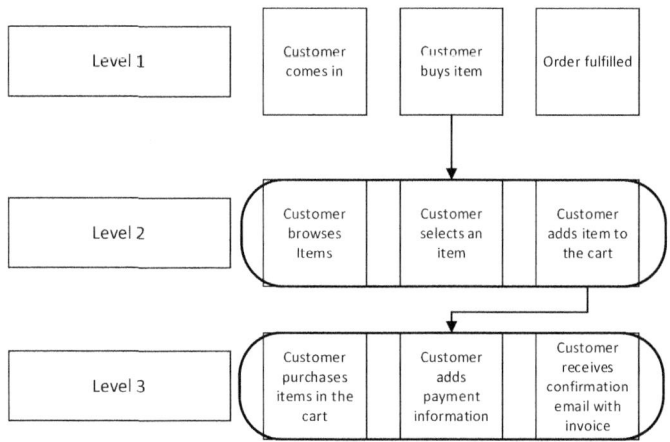

Figure 26: Process Levels

Start from the highest concept in levels, take each step and drill deeper, breaking down the steps into more fine-grained steps. This is particularly useful in limited-time scenarios when you need to produce something fast.

Business Analysis Techniques and Business Process Improvement | 95

Some drawing applications have more attractive shapes than others, making a chart much easier to read and interpret. In this example, only basic shapes are used. Start with three things.

- Identify the process by naming it and listing the owner's name.
- List all entities/functions/actors in the process.
- From the activities, start listing all the activities based on their nature.

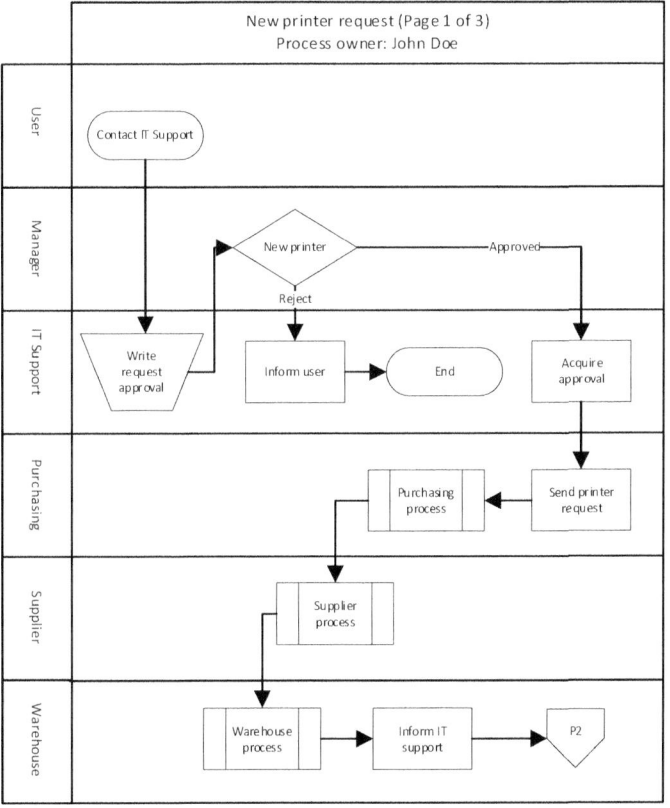

Figure 27: Completed Swimlane Flowchart, Page 1

96 | Business Analysis and Process Modeling Guidebook

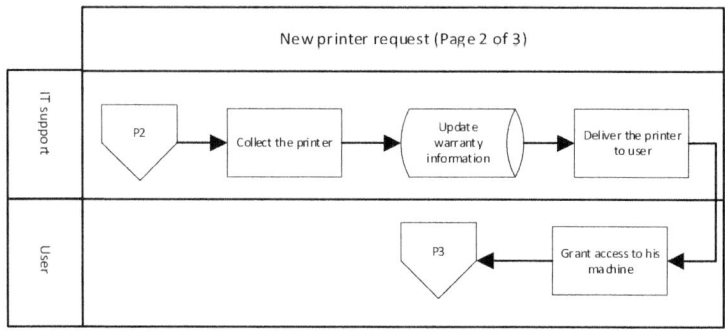

Figure 28: Completed Swimlane Flowchart, Page 2

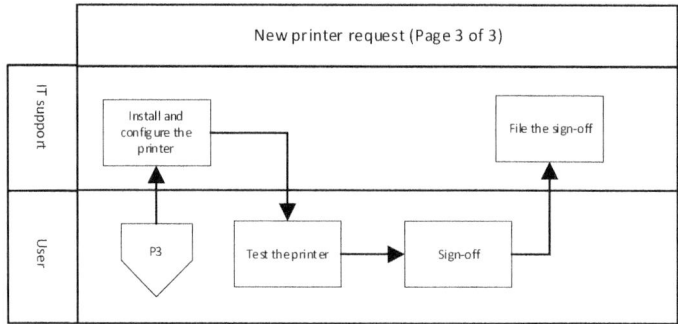

Figure 29: Completed Swimlane Flowchart, Page 3

At this point, the process is well known, and you shed light on it. If you are building an application, this would be the final step. But if this is a documentation project to improve the internal process, this will be the first step.

Chapter 8: Process Assessment and Standardization

In the previous chapters, you learned how to analyze business requirements and build a business process. In many cases, this would be enough to deliver a successful project. But sometimes, you do all of that to build a practice, not a project. In this case, you need to go further in the investigation.

Standardized practices generate predictable outcomes and benefits the business can rely on to take risks in other areas. Every business has a risk tolerance. If the process results vary, it is considered risky because the business cannot predict the waste, the volume, or the benefits, among other things. Standardizing the process and system will lead to a more stable environment and more stable revenue. This, in turn, will allow the business to take risks in more critical areas such as innovation.

The first step is performing the assessment. Here are the benefits of an assessment:

- When you know what's missing, you can plan the next steps.
- During the assessment, people will be exposed more to the process, clarifying the steps.
- The assessment gives a sense of importance to the processes.
- The assessment opens up discussions for new projects.

The assessment idea is to identify the strong and weak areas in the practices to guide the organization toward more standardized practices. The building block of any practice is the process, and assessing the process is the starting point. There are two types of processes: standardized and unstandardized.

In **standardized processes**, input, output, and path are well defined.

Unstandardized processes have defined input and output but uneven steps with undefined limits.

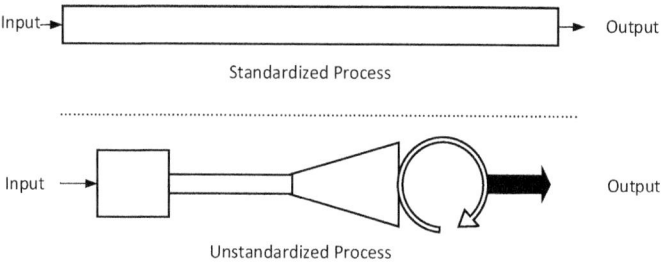

Figure 30: Standardized vs. Unstandardized Process

Both processes are reliable and produce the desired output at the end. The difference between the two is the level of predictable outputs generated. For example, standardized processes and practices generate an output within a specific range. In an unstandardized process or practice, the output will vary because you will usually have different elements in each segment. Figure 31 illustrates this example:

- A process has very good customer service receiving requests.
- But it has only one Level 2 agent (that deals with this request, creating a bottleneck.
- Afterward, the process needs to depend on searches of changes with a different number of people to determine the source of the complaint.
- Finally, it goes through a loop (trial and error) until the desired output is approved.

In traditional process modeling, you will see the process and even draw it, but you will not see the shape of the practice as a whole. Determining this shape is the role of the assessment. This is referred to as a simple assessment. It is not a comprehensive assessment and should not take long (a few weeks).

The process assessment ensures that proper documentation and evidence exist for the practices and processes implementation.

Additionally, policies, actions, and documentation must exist for each level of work before the practice can advance to the next level.

This chapter will introduce you to the concept from a high-level perspective and show you how such an assessment should flow.

To assess the maturity, follow a process called appraisal, which measures the maturity of the current process and determines what's missing. Maturity indicates whether a process is ill-managed at one end of the scale, fully optimized at the other, or somewhere in between.

This assessment should never be conducted right after the process implementation. Wait until the new practice is widely accepted, and then perform the analysis. Sometimes the initial business process did not exist before, so allow people to work with it to understand it better and build the practice around it. Go directly for assessment only if you are a consultant for an organization and want to highlight the gaps.

A service assessment can be subjective because it is tied to the perspectives of the people taking it. Even so, an assessment will indicate where a process falls in performance measures; and it can reveal process shortcomings.

This assessment is inspired by an appraisal strategy known as Capability Maturity Model Integration (CMMI), although the approach has been greatly simplified and modified to fit this book's objective.

Laying Down Foundation

Decide on the framework you will follow. The words "process" and "practice" are used loosely in many frameworks, but you should pick one framework and measure based on it; for example, Information Technology Infrastructure Library (ITIL) 4 has 34 practice areas, and CMMI has 24 process areas. You don't have to do them all. You only have to pick which practice or process area is closest to your organization and start measuring based on that. You could end up with part ITIL, part CMMI, and some from IT4IT and The Open Group Architecture Framework (TOGAF). Though a hybrid model will not produce the optimal results, it will create very good results until the organization can develop and optimize its framework to its own needs and business objectives.

Now the assessment usually takes based on three verticals. Let's take service operations in IT as an example. Let's say you decided to use ITIL 3 as your measurement point, and you will evaluate the practice based on a few processes only.

People: the team, the skills, the team capacity

Process: event management, access management, request fulfillment, incident management, problem management

Technology: the tools and software used

Each of the three processes will have its own maturity level.

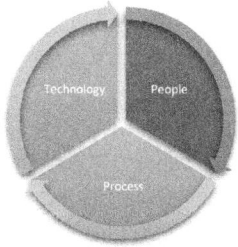

So always build the framework you will measure against to determine the practice itself. If you are doing this for a single process (such as problem management only), take the best practice guidebook and measure based on that.

Step 1: Initial Plan for the Assessment

Understand that an in-depth assessment will consume lots of time, effort, and money. This is a high-level plan to make sure management knows the precise requirements.

1. **Define scope**: Define where you must go to find objects related to the assessment. For example, can you trace the process inside IT? Or will you pursue other areas as well, such as the human resource and finance departments? The model's built-in Step 0 will significantly influence what can be measured and what will be skipped. Remember you

are measuring things in three ways: the people using the process, the technology they are using (the tools), and the process itself (the activities).
2. **State the objective**: It may be to reduce costs, for example, or improve quality and speed the process.
3. **Identify what data will be collected and how it will be collected:** This will be accomplished through interviews, questionnaires, prototyping, presentations, roundtables, surveys, etc.
4. **Identify team members**: Identify the participants and team members performing the data collection and describe their roles.
5. **Identify script questions**: This is an important but time-consuming step. If the data is gathered incorrectly, the result could distort findings from all other areas of the assessment.
6. **Identify any constraints**: Identify access and availability for all required resources, team members, and facilities.
7. **Determine cost and scheduling**: Estimate costs for the people participating in the assessment and for any equipment. Consider the expected duration of the assessment and provide a schedule for the availability of resources and facilities.
8. **Perform risk analysis and management**:
    - Identify risks (personal, logistical, technical, scheduling).
    - Develop mitigation plans for critical risks.
9. **State expected outputs**: ratings, reports, recommendations, findings, strengths, and weaknesses

Some expect a simple number from the process assessment. In many cases, this can be a high-level representation of process maturity. But to gain greater meaning, findings should include associated documentation explaining why one process delivers a disappointing rating, but another process merits an optimal rating. Having one number per practice (people, process, and technology) score and a total aggregate organization score could persuade the management team to implement the needed changes.

Once the initial assessment plan is created, proceed to formally approve the plan and secure the needed resources.

Step 2: Assemble the Team

Based on the assessment size, one team could be sufficient, or multiple teams might be required. One final note about this: internal assessment tends to be a bit optimistic because colleagues assess one another, and they care about the relationships. It's always best to get someone from outside the organization to give a realistic view of the status. If this is not possible, try to get someone from another branch.

Team Leader

Pick an experienced assessment team leader who knows the business and has multiple skill sets across the process in question. The individual must learn about ITIL or the framework created (the ability to align IT with business needs), PMP or proficient in productivity measurement), or a similar high-level capability.

These are the core requirements for a team leader:

- Maintain management commitment for the assessment process
- Ensure that team members know their roles and responsibilities
- Is not the owner of any process

Team Members

- The team size will scale up based on assessment requirements. (Usually, there are three people plus the team leader.) Each team member must know about the framework created in Step 0 or at least possess its core knowledge.
- Each must have experience in and be familiar with the process in question.
- Each must have excellent communication skills.
- Part of the team should be outside of IT.
- No person who wrote all or part of the original process may be on the team. One team member must serve as project coordinator to arrange access, facilities, and interviews; manage schedules;

and request documents. The project coordinator will also file the documents.

Team Preparation

1. Conduct team building. (Refer to Ch. 4.)
2. The team leader should ensure that all team members are aware of the objectives.
3. Conduct a workshop to ensure that all team members know their roles and that there are no knowledge gaps.
4. Brief all members on the purpose of maturity during the process workshop.
5. Teach all team members how to interview. Role playing can advance this skill.
6. Arrange an assessment kickoff.

Step 3: Executing the Plan

Once the initial plan is authorized and all information on availability and constraints is gathered, refine the plan. Start by collecting evidence that describes the process or objective, inventorying all the evidence supplied, and determining the gaps. This will aid in establishing any additional information that needs to be collected. This initial collection is usually done via email.

For example, the request could be: "Please provide the input and output of the activity (describe the activity). The acceptable formats are (files, screenshots, emails, etc.)

As mentioned earlier, you should conduct the assessment after you build the process. This would be a very short assessment if the process does not exist. So, the assessment starting point is the flowcharts or swimlane. In the flowchart, write the process owner's name on top (the first stakeholder interview), then gather the evidence for each activity in the flowchart from him or from whomever he points out.

Sometimes the evidence can be a verbal confirmation, although written evidence is preferred for this key effort. Once all evidence is in hand, take inventory to track precisely what has been collected. This can become the basis for a deeper evidence dive.

Create an evidence tracking sheet to maintain a list of everything that is found.

Examples of evidence: Sign-off sheets, invoices, booklets, a demonstration of a person going through the process. All are considered evidence of the process.

Item name	Item type	Item number
License certificate	certificate	EV1
Mail system hardware	invoice	EV2
Software PO	invoice	EV3
Email flowchart	flowchart	EV4
Email support incident	Sign-off	EV5
System design	design	EV6
Email upgrade form	change request	EV7
Business case	design	EV8

Table 19: Evidence Sheet Example

After building the evidence sheet, categorize the evidence into several groups:

- **Strong evidence**: something that strongly demonstrates that a process is in place. This can be, for example, a process chart with relevant document.
- **Weak evidence**: a document related to a process. This might be a process change request or an article that shows knowledge of a service.
- **Not relevant**
- **Conflicting or inconsistent**

Item name	Item type	Item number	Strength
License certificate	certificate	EV1	weak
Mail system hardware	invoice	EV2	weak
Software PO	invoice	EV3	not relevant
Email flowchart	flowchart	EV4	strong
Email support incident	Sign-off	EV5	strong
System design	design	EV6	strong
Email upgrade form	change request	EV7	strong
Business case	design	EV8	strong

Table 20: Categorized Evidence Sheet Example

Business Analysis Techniques and Business Process Improvement | 105

The idea here is to ensure that the process produces the same results and that no steps are skipped or corners cut.

Once the categorized evidence sheet is built, start building the service-to-evidence mapping sheets. Build four sheets for each service, one per evidence category. The categories are the ones selected earlier, when we decided to use ITIL3. The service life cycle in ITIL3 is Strategy, Design, Transition, Operation.

Strong evidence	Flowchart	Sign-off	Design	Change request
Strategy			EV8	
Design	EV4			
Transition	EV4		EV6	EV7
Operation	EV4	EV5		

Table 21: Service-to-evidence Mapping Example

Initial Findings Review

Give the plan a final review before actually starting the assessment. Review the following factors:

- Team readiness
- Data readiness
- Logistics
- Risk plan
- Data collection (Update any evidence collection still needed to create a complete picture.)

The Kickoff Meeting

The kickoff meeting puts all participants on notice that the assessment is starting. The meeting can be face to face, via video or telephone conference, or even by email. Use the meeting to refresh participants on what is expected from them and to confirm their availability. The audience for this meeting is the process owners, identified stakeholders, and the assessment team.

Examination Phase

Examine the data collected during the planning phase and update the interview question list accordingly. Once the examination phase starts, a freezing process begins. This means no changes to the process. The assessment must finish as early as possible. During the examination, the team will determine whether the data collected is useful and to what degree.

Start with the data collection method selected in the planning phase. In the examination phase, the team does not finish until sufficient data is collected to judge the state of the process under assessment. The volume of data required is determined in the planning phase.

This phase is done through everyone who interacts with the process, not the owner, to judge whether the data and evidence provided from the owner is the actual process that is happening or perceive by the other stakeholders.

The examination is done in workshops and one-on-one interviews, with these objectives:

- Confirm that the evidence collected in the initial phase is the standard input/outputs
- Confirm the missing evidence is missing, and no process is in place. Sometimes part of the process doesn't produce evidence, or the evidence is part of the people completing the process.

Maintaining Collected Data

Whatever the team collects or takes note of must be maintained and verified. It is recommended that someone on the team maintain the flowcharts and collect all the data as the team gathers it. This is called a data process. It involves a review, and it tags the data correctly to group it.

As in previous steps, perform a gap analysis. It will be updated with new evidence if it satisfies the assessor. Use a tool such as a tracking table.

Business Analysis Techniques and Business Process Improvement | 107

Service area	Strong evidence	Weak evidence	Not relevant	Conflicting/ inconsistent
Strategy	3	2	0	1
Design	2	1	0	1
Transition	5	4	2	0
Operation	8	1	1	0

Table 22: Collected Evidence Table Example

Once the team updates the tracking table, a new gap report will be created; the gap report will document both the demonstrated maturity level and the desired, expected level.

Each process has three categories:

- Fully implemented practice
- Partially implemented practice with notes on what's missing
- Needed practice

At this point, the team should have collected all the information, facts, and evidence required; no area should still be missing evidence.

Start the verification process to make sure collected data is sufficient and nothing is missing.

Generate Findings

It is time for the team to agree on each process:

1. Review the reference model.
2. Summarize the strength of the process. (Strength is above and beyond expectation, for example.)
3. Summarize the weakness (any lack of implementation in one or more practice areas).

In the finding, the process area should be one of the following with a description of any gap:

- **Fully implemented**: No weakness. Evidence found in the process is adequate to the requirements and to the reference model.
- **Largely implemented**: Comparable to fully implemented but has weakness.

- **Partially implemented**: Data is missing or contradictory. Weaknesses are found.
- **Not implemented**: Lots of data is missing, and weakness is found.
- **Not yet**: The unit is too small or too simple to have a complicated process. (The steps are limited).

Data Validation

The last step is to validate the data collected from the members of the organization.

Only people who participated in data gathering may participate in the validation. To validate findings, use these tools:

- **Presentation and groups**: Always use the same seniority level in the same meeting so people will speak their minds. Complaining about something with a senior in the room might be considered an escalation.
- **Survey**: Surveys represent one-way communication. Use them to complement other methods of gathering feedback.

Generate Results

At this point, all the facts are available. It is time to understand the rating process.

Understand Levels

Levels are a generic evaluation of a process that could integrate into the framework built earlier. Levels are how organizations understand the path to improvement for a set of processes. There are two improvement paths:

- **Capability levels**: Consider each process separately. Incrementally improved processes correspond to a single process or a group of processes.
- **Maturity levels**: The master process incrementally addresses a set of processes and how they function together.

Those levels correspond to the following approaches to process improvement:

Business Analysis Techniques and Business Process Improvement | 109

- **Continuous**: Using the continuous approach, progress toward a higher capability level will occur by developing one or more processes without other processes in the group keeping pace.
- **Staged**: Using the staged approach, the process will achieve a higher maturity level only as all other processes also are upgraded to the desired level.

Think of it this way: Capability levels focus on one specific process area, while maturity levels focus on multiprocess areas.

The levels in each are 1 to 5. (There is a Level 0, which represents an incomplete.)

Level	Capability levels	Maturity levels
0	Incomplete	-
1	Performed	Initial
2	Managed	Managed
3	Defined	Defined
4	-	Quantitatively Managed
5	-	Optimized

Table 23: Service Levels

There is no point in trying to optimize a master process for Level 0 if the capabilities of the building process are incomplete.

Once the process reaches Level 3 in each process area, the focus will be on how the process works to provide value. This is why Levels 4 and 5 use only overall process grouping (staged).

In the diagram below, capability levels are applied to Processes 1, 2, 3, and to Processes A, B, C. Maturity levels, by contrast, apply to the master process, which has multiple subprocesses (1, 2, 3, and A, B, C).

110 | Business Analysis and Process Modeling Guidebook

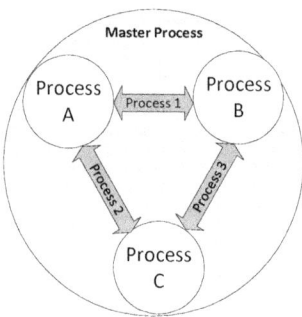

Figure 31: Master Process

Capability Levels

- **Capability Level 0, Incomplete**: This process is neither performed nor fully implemented.
- **Capability Level 1, Performed**: A performed process will produce a result or a specific goal and is considered a high-level accomplishment. This process may be lost over time or abandoned during a period of stress.
- **Capability Level 2, Managed**: This is a performed process but with a policy attached. The policy will ensure that these are present:
    - Skilled employees
    - Necessary resources
    - Stakeholder involvement
    - Monitoring
    - A process control factor
    - Review and evaluation

  The policy's existence will ensure that its practices will remain unchanged in a time of stress.
- **Capability Level 3, Defined**: This refers to a managed process tailored to the needs of the work. Level 3 processes are typically described more rigorously than those in Level 2. They spell out the following:
    - Purpose
    - Inputs
    - Entry criteria
    - Activities
    - Roles

Business Analysis Techniques and Business Process Improvement | 111

- Measures
- Verification steps
- Outputs
- Exit criteria

Processes at this level are managed more proactively.

Maturity Level

- **Maturity Level 1, Initial**: Usually this level comes into play due to people who work in an organization, not because of the process. The problem elements may signal, Lack of a stable environment, Operations that go over budget or an insufficient schedule and Process abandonment in a time of crisis.
- **Maturity Level 2, Managed**: This level is the organization's foundation as a service provider.
    - Work groups define services delivery as follows:
        - Planned
        - Monitored
        - Controlled
        - Having quality control
    - Agreements are established with customers, and contracts are made, such as service level agreements (SLAs) and operational level agreements (OLAs).
    - Configuration management and quality assurance processes are rooted in the organization's core.
    - Capabilities exist to measure performance.
    - The processes, work activities, and services meet the following criteria:
        - Managed
        - Executed with enough resources
        - Have assigned responsibilities
        - Have trained people
        - Include configuration management
        - Involve stakeholders who periodically monitor and control the processes
    - Performance reports are shared with higher management.
    - Existing practices are retained during times of stress.
- **Maturity Level 3, Defined**:
    - This level uses a defined process for managing work.

- Applies best practices (service continuity, incident resolution, and prevention) to the master process.
- Validates requirements to meet customer expectations.
- The process is well understood, and process parameters are defined.
- Processes are described in detail. The following details are included:
  - Purpose
  - Inputs
  - Entry criteria
  - Activities
  - Roles
  - Measures
  - Verification steps
  - Outputs
  - Exit criteria
  - More proactive management
- **Maturity Level 4, Quantitatively Managed**: At this level, the primary focus is "understanding and controlling the performance of a process and subprocess."
  - A critical distinction between Maturity Levels 3 and 4 is the predictability of process performance (how close the forecast is to real life.)
  - KPIs are set for quality and process performance objectives.
  - The KPIs are based on the needs of the customer, end users, and the organization.
- **Maturity Level 5, Optimizing**: In Level 5, the primary focus is the organization—specifically, how to improve the overall performance of the organization, how to innovate, and how to close the gaps and shortfalls in performance.

Moving through the Levels

To begin a move, the organization must have control of its systems. Any organization that wishes to move forward cannot skip levels or cut corners. If maturity is not sufficiently stable, the effort may be ripped apart in its first test. Moving ahead means mastering every level. Processes without the proper foundation can fail when they are needed most—under stress.

This approach applies to a specific process within capability levels, and it applies to the master process group as it rises through maturity levels. All the maturity level processes should perform at their best before advancement to the next level can occur.

Key points:

- Don't move on to the next level until the current level is well established. With every new level, commit to remaining for six months to a year to give the processes time to demonstrate stability and dependability. Develop an improvement road map with milestones.
- This guidance applies to capability levels as well as maturity levels. You will end up with two levels for each process, one for the process group and one for the single process.
- A single process cannot pass to Level 4, but the process group can.
- To move to a higher maturity level, develop all subprocesses in the group.

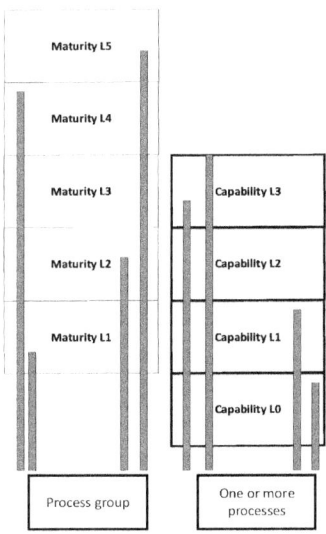

Figure 32: Moving through the Levels

To achieve each level, the process, whether master or a single process, must earn the following in the three vectors (people, process, and technology):

Level 1: Incomplete and Performed Process/Initial Process

- Achieve a specific goal, the process of transforming identifiable input into output.
- Perform a specific practice.

This process can be informal, without any document. The process earns the level once it finishes all the sublevel goals and practices

Level 2: Managed Process

The process is presented as a managed process. Each of the goals of the level is divided into sublevels for easier measurement.

Level 2.1 Core of the process

- Establish and maintain a policy for planning and performing the process.
- Define the expectation of higher management.

Level 2.2 Plan the Process

- Have a process plan that includes the following:
  - Process description
  - Requirements for the services of the process
  - Specific objectives of the process and its results
  - Dependencies among the activities, work products, and services of the process resources
  - Training requirements
  - Activities for monitoring and controlling the process
  - Evaluation of the process
  - Review of activities for the process and subcomponents
  - Review of the plan with relevant stakeholders
  - Agreement of relevant stakeholders

Level 2.3 Provide Resources

- Provide enough resources for performing the process and final service.

Level 2.4 Assign Responsibilities

- Create a responsibility and authority matrix.
- Ensure there is accountability for performing the process and achieving specific results (milestones).
- Verify that the service team understands and accepts its responsibilities.

Level 2.5 Training

- Conduct training as needed for users performing or supporting the process.

Level 2.6 Control Outputs

- Monitor and control progress to maintain consistent output and quality levels.

Level 2.7 Involve Stakeholders

- Identify process stakeholders.
- Involve relevant stakeholders.

Level 2.8 Monitoring the Process

- Monitor and control the process in accordance with the plan.
- Take corrective action in the event of any deviation.
- Do the following periodically:
    1. Evaluate actual performance vs. planned.
    2. Evaluate actual results vs. planned.
    3. Review the process (inputs and outputs) with the process owner.
    4. Identify and evaluate any deviation from the plan.
    5. Identify mismatch in the plan for performance vs. the execution of the process.

6. Take corrective action when requirements and objectives are not satisfied.

Most monitoring software can perform all of these activities by setting a benchmark for the process and generating daily reports that are shared with management and process owners.

Level 2.9 Evaluate the Process

- Ensure that the implemented process is functioning as planned and follows the process description, standards, and procedures.
- Correct any deviation.

Level 2.10 Review Status

- Review process inputs and outputs with management and resolve any issues. Secure resources as needed.

Final Results

Each process should have evidence covering each block of the service reference model; otherwise, it is a weak service, and further development is required. The report typically contains this information:

- Assessment data
- Final findings with context data
- Assessment plan and the items collected (artifacts)
- Recommendation and improvement report
- Recommendations (tied to identified weakness)
- An improvement action plan

Deliver the final report and recommendations to the sponsor. Arrange a presentation session for executives (top management and key stakeholders). Privately rehearse the presentation before the formal delivery. This will help to avoid surprises and refine presentation pacing.

Business Analysis Techniques and Business Process Improvement | 117

The outcome is to show an as-is business model, whether or not the process is stable and mature. Because from this point forward, you need to start optimizing the process.

Remediation

Now you have a gap between the desired outcome and the objective. The first step is to start building what's missing based on the generated finding. Each practice leader should drive the process improvement by asking his or her team to fill in the gaps. The business analyst's role will be to guide people on building what's missing and performing progress reviews. The evidence created by the stakeholders should be integrated into the evidence sheets and included for later evaluation. After this, find the integration points, build a capability, and standardize these steps. This will lead to more of a streamlined practice.

Chapter 9: Process Improvement

This chapter will explain the meaning of process improvement and how statistical process control (SPC) will provide a more stable and dependable process. The primary concern of process improvement is having a predictable output and predictability in the activities of the process. The process could be Level 3 with significant evidence, yet the outputs range needs to be improved, and the steps could also be improved.

What Is Process Improvement?

Process improvement is all about finding what your organization uses to generate revenue and doing it better, cheaper, faster, and with higher quality. But before that, you need to work with management to address a few obstacles that will stop you early on.

- **Lack of consistency of purpose:** This usually happens if no vision exists.
- **Emphasis on short-term profits:** This happens when operations take control. In this case, try to get 1 to 5 percent investment in strategic initiatives.
- **Unstable management (unclear direction):** Avoid this pitfall by working with management to define a "north star."
- **Decisions based on "hunches," not figures:** Show the benefits of the figures and how they can expose a lot more opportunities.
- **A reactive mindset, not a proactive one.** Say, for example, a business is spending lots of money trying to restore customer satisfaction after customers are dissatisfied. Instead, document the losses and how the losses could be avoided in the future.
- **Money spent on services that can be avoided:** One example would be lawsuits. Generate lesson learned.

To cure these six problems that exist in many organizations, set a regular meeting with the management, with the primary objective of improving the company's profitability. Try to address the issues with one of the counterstrategies mentioned.

Before deciding on the process improvement, you have to document the process, understand it, and determine possible improvement areas.

You will be amazed at how many redundant steps and unnecessary loops show up when you document the process. If you are not seeing it and measuring it, you might think things are OK when they are not. Moreover, you will not notice until the situation gets terrible. Every critical activity in the process needs to be measured. A baseline (the normal) needs to be determined. If there is a problem, target that specific problem and solve it.

Moreover, measure whether your solution improves the outcome of the process.

Measuring all activities would be overkill and would consume lots of resources and time. Start by analyzing the process outputs. Are they within the normal range? Then begin investigating backward to find odd output. To determine odd output vs. normal, try comparing it to industry standard or the organization numbers in the past year for the same period.

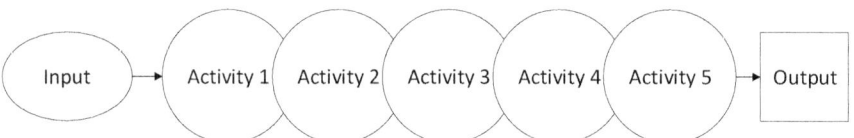

Figure 33: Activity Chain

If it's the first year of analysis, the process can improve using common sense and nothing else. Some institutes sell industry-standard information, but these are generic numbers and help only if the case is extreme. It will not assist in gaining a competitive advantage. The only way to improve is to benchmark against the organization itself.

However, a first step to improving a process is simplifying and reducing steps to achieve the outcome. After drawing the process steps using a flowchart or swimlane, ask the following questions:

1. Can any steps be deleted?
2. Can any steps be automated or partially automated?

3. Can any steps be combined?
4. Can any steps alter to be performed by one person instead of two?
5. Is it possible to run activities in parallel?

Answering these questions will open up many optimization projects that will generate value for the organization without much investment.

Statistical Process Control (SPC)

Process control is finding the ideal condition of the activities. If any of these activities changed from ideal status, the process outcomes would be less desirable.

Figure 34: QCT Triangle

Maybe the activities will be focused on speed, cost, quality, or balance. The idea is to find the spot on this triangle that suits the company best. There is no good or bad position. The business's location is determined to fulfill a specific market niche by using a specific mix of resources.

The difficult spot is the exact middle; this means 100% quality with 0% waste (or cost 100%) and 100% on time. The middle is almost impossible, and if possible, it will be expensive and resource-intensive. QCT Triangle means there is an almost infinite number of possibilities where the process will be performing ideally for the organization. The numbers on the triangle are to demonstrate the concept only. Point 1 represents high quality at a high cost with slow output. This is Apple, for example.

The problem always is changing this point from one position to another. DevOps, agile, and cloud help organizations change their position in the triangle quickly to achieve better results for the business. Without the three, it's difficult to move the organization's dot location, but organizations can select and change the position according to market demands. Otherwise, it might fall short or move too late to a location that the market already moved away from (like Nokia with smartphones or Kodak with the digital camera).

The issue with most examples is that they talk about a final product but rarely about services. When it comes to lean, products and services are both the same. Instead of the production line to create a product, you have servers, people, and devices.

This means products or services are the outcome; it will be the email message coming out of the user machine, the meal in a restaurant, or a product from a supermarket. The product concept is applied to *all* aspects, including services.

First, understand quality, cost, and time to decide where the process should be.

Quality

To have quality, you need two things:

- Prevention cost, prevention time
- Failure cost

Prevention Cost/Time

This is the cost and time consumed to ensure that every activity is done up to the standard. The more quality demanded, the more cost and time are required.

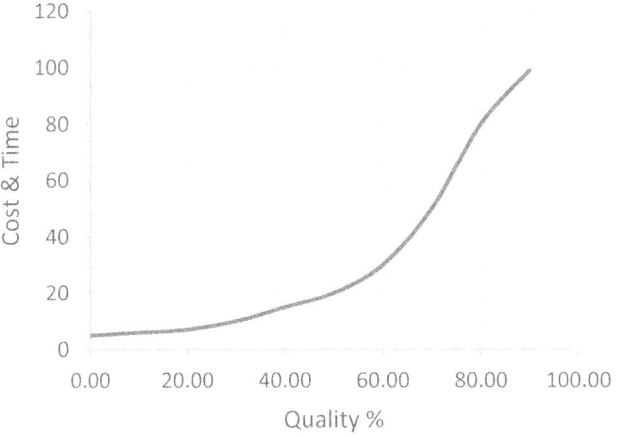

Figure 35: Prevention Cost/Time

Failure Cost

The cost of time wasted due to low quality (rework again and waste resources because first attempt was not up to the standard). The lower the quality, the more expensive it is due to rework or even a lawsuit.

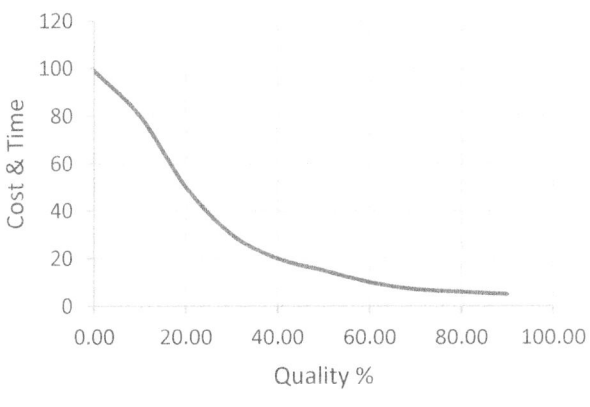

Figure 36: Failure Cost

Now if you apply both graphs, you end up with this:

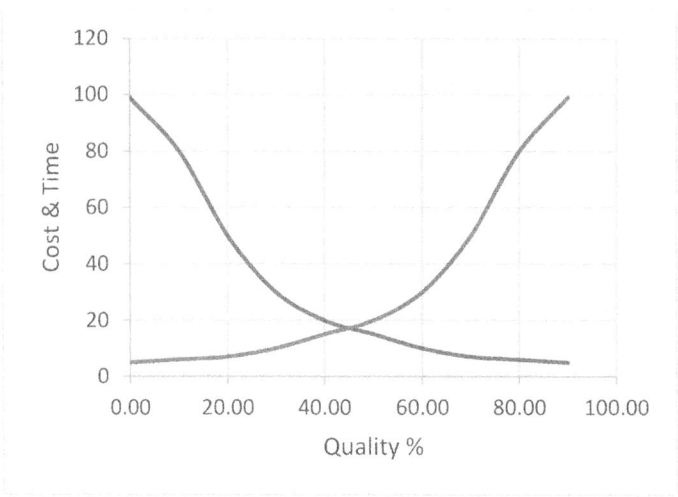

Figure 37: Prevention Cost/Time & Failure Cost

The lowest cost is where both curves intersect, but unfortunately, it's the commodity's point. The point of the commodity means you will have average quality. In today's business, this is not a good choice since most companies that focus on quality outlast the companies focusing on cost (think Apple). Always try to stay in the golden zone (Zone 1). If you go for Zone 2 (the gray zone), the failure cost will outmatch any profit realized from cutting corners.

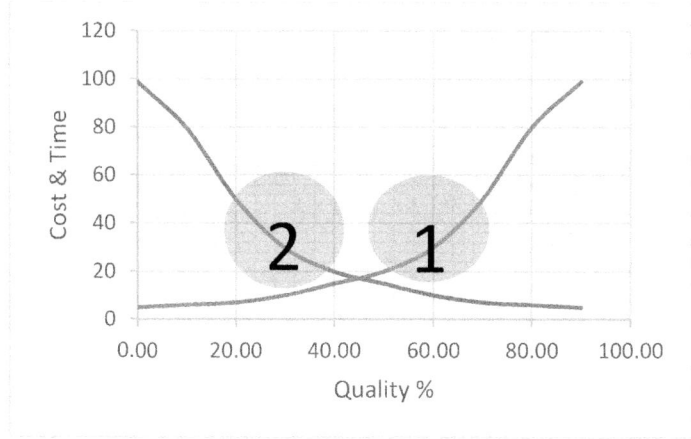

Figure 38: Golden and Gray Zones

Now that you understand quality, it's time to decide where quality needs to be. Selecting quality levels is done by calculating the failure and prevention costs. After gathering marketing and production data, the organization decides the quality equals 70 percent

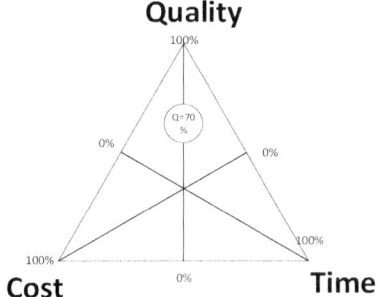

Figure 39: Quality Score

Cost

To reduce cost, you need to cut several things such as the following:

- **Waste**: Waste of time, waste of materials, and waste of facilities
- **Defects**: Any defects in the product that render it useless or cause the customer to return it
- **Overproduction**: Units overproduced and waiting in stock, store cost
- **Waiting**: The time wasted waiting for products, half a product waiting for the next step
- **Not utilizing talent**: Any employee with a skill not used. To have anyone utilizing only part of their talent is a massive waste in organizations today.
- **Transportation**: Any movement of people, products, or anything needs to be optimized for the least transportation time
- **Inventory excess**: Raw materials, work in progress, finished materials. It should not be in your inventory if it's not for a customer.
- **Motion waste:** The effort in people and the wear and tear of machines
- **Excess processing**: The overdesign of the process to things the customer does not care about

To calculate the cost, combine all the above waste (if you have them on the product or service) and reach a total number:

(Cost / Cost + Waste)

Let's assume it's 70 percent.

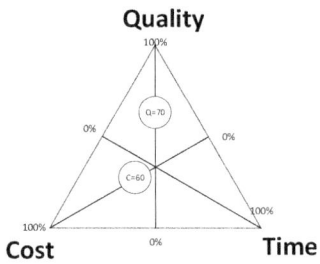

Figure 40: Cost Score

Time

Lead time is the time it takes for the first product or service to go through the entire set of activities. If one activity causes a constraint or a bottleneck (queues), time is wasted. To save time:

1. Have a better layout to move things between activities and processes faster.
2. For each queue that is a bottleneck, try to eliminate it or reduce the queue.

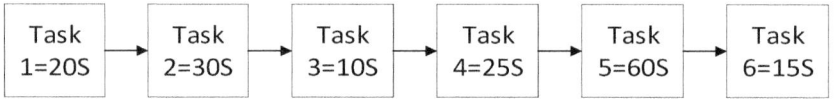

Figure 41: Task Duration

In Figure 42, the process will produce only sixty units per hour (the slowest task N.5). A queue will form between tracks four and five, while task six will be underutilized.

So how long for inputs to become outputs? Five minutes and fifteen seconds (315 seconds) because the queue moves only once every sixty seconds. So Task 1 will have to wait for a new task for sixty seconds for the processed task input to become outputs, inputs to Task 2, etc.

Enhancing Tasks 2 or 4 will waste capacity. The only improvement to the line will be to reduce Task 5. To which extent you plan to enhance the time is dependent on the demand. In our example

time = bottlenecks / total process time

so time = 60 / 315, or 19%

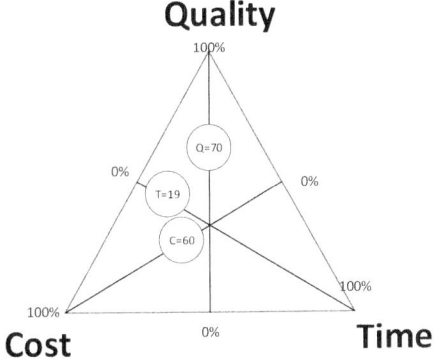

Figure 42: Time Score

Now to find the position of the organization process in the triangle, we draw three lines. Each line bisecting circles.

1. We draw a line splitting each circle into half and land on the center of a previously drawn line.
2. The intersection point is the position.

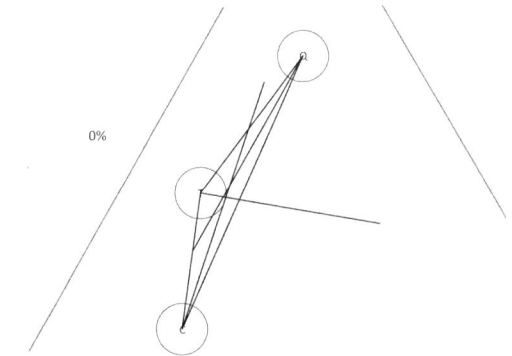

Figure 43: Intersection Point

Clean things up a bit, and you end with this:

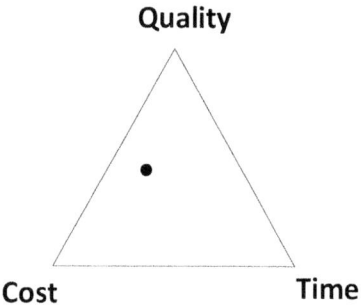

Figure 44: Position

Adjusting the Position

The whole idea of finding the location on the triangle is to show that changing it is not an easy task and might unpredictably impact other aspects. Let's take capacity and demand as an example. In our example, suppose we try to reduce cost by reducing the number of call center agents. In that case, there is no point in serving more than one person per sixty seconds as it will pile up before the bottleneck, and our total capacity is sixty people per hour (one each sixty seconds). If our demand is only fifty units per hour (evenly spaced), there is no point in improving. But if our demand is ninety units, it's worth investing in improving the current bottleneck enough to serve the required demand.

If your demand is not evenly spaced, which is typically the case, measure the demand fluctuation and reserve the capacity to serve it. (Thirty minutes, a request of forty units, and five units in total in another hour. The average of the two is below sixty per hour, but both are different orders, and we cannot rely on averages in this case.) In this example

queue length (not evenly spaced) = utilization / (1 – utilization)

So because the forty units are considered 66% utilization of the line,

66 / (100 – 66) = 1.94 queue length

and the average wait time is the the average unit wait time multiplied by the queue length:

60 x 1.94 = 116.5 seconds.

Business Analysis Techniques and Business Process Improvement | 129

To eliminate the queues (to get the queue to 1, which is the person or unit being served), make the utilization 50 percent, which means double the capacity to eliminate waiting time. This is the capacity required to reduce the queue size.

The problem is that the organization needs to reduce cost by increasing utilization, and customers need lower waiting times, so you have to find the balance between the two.

When optimizing a process, don't cut it to the bone to make it 99.99 percent utilized. Doing so will generate undereffect (hidden effect) to the customers and impact the organization in the long run. Process optimization takes time to understand the hidden effect's impact.

What if a delay happened in Task 1 or 2? The delay would not cause an impact. It would only leave a gap in production, but since these tasks are faster than the bottleneck, it will catch up once the issue is resolved. This is considered a buffer. This also should be calculated based on business requirements. For example, calculate the buffer if Task 1 were delayed.

For Task 5 to finish the queue (the 4 units created by tasks 1-4) it takes four minutes, and for a unit to reach Task 5, it will take eighty-five seconds (the total time required for Tasks 1-4), so the buffer will be

$$240 - 85 = 155 \text{ seconds (or 2.58 minutes)}$$

This is the time allowed for Task 1 to have an issue without impacting the line.

It is all about relaxing the constraints to improve the overall outputs of the process by fixing the bottleneck, adjusting the buffer, and reducing the waste.

Best Practices for the Bottleneck

- Make sure it never breaks down.
- Never run out of supplies.
- Never supply it with damaged or defective parts.

The bottleneck could be a highly skilled individual, a machine, or a system. The same concept applies. Sometimes the bottleneck could be an Interactive voice response system (IVR) or a core switch or even a system administrator with specific knowledge to do something.

Understanding Process Outcomes

All these readings come from a monitoring system. The tools even render the distribution of data collected. Understand how it is done manually to understand what you see and what it means. This also helps define the limits for the process and the activities inside the process.

Outputs are where statistics come in. To understand this, when you see the process outputs (or activities) multiple times, there are three options:

- Perfect scenario
- Type 1 (no grouping of results)
- Type 2 (grouped results)

Perfect Scenario

In this scenario, the process generates the same results each time, which is the ideal.

Figure 45: Perfect Scenario

Type 1 (No Grouping of Results)

In this process, outputs widely vary with each process run. The process is unpredictable. In statistical terms, the results have too much variation. To deal with that, we take sample readings and do our plot. This will give us an idea of the type of process we do have.

Figure 46: Type 1 (No Grouping of Results)

Type 2 (Grouped Results)

The process outcomes vary but within a predictable range. In this scenatio, the average is drifted.

Figure 47: Type 2 (Results Grouped)

The improvement idea is to take Type 1 and make it Type 2. For the process of Type 2, try to shift it to the ideal scenario. In some cases,

132 | Business Analysis and Process Modeling Guidebook

we cannot reach the ideal situation, so we decide on a variation limit we think is OK and improve based on that.

What if your process was going well, and suddenly things started to get worse? How do you intervene?

First, recalculate your sample size to ensure your data is accurate. However, as a rule of thumb, 1.2 periods are required, where the period is the typical reporting period (usually weekly). This means waiting eight to nine days to determine whether things had gone bad in the process. If the process was an ideal or near-ideal state, things are not falling out of control yet. It's still at a predictable level.

This is the process (solid bars represent the ideal scenario):

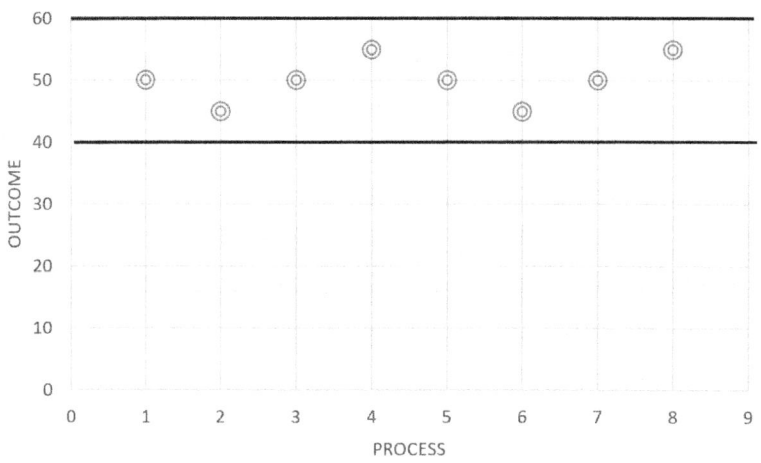

Figure 48: Statistical Process Control (median moving range-MMR)

The process turned into this:

Business Analysis Techniques and Business Process Improvement | 133

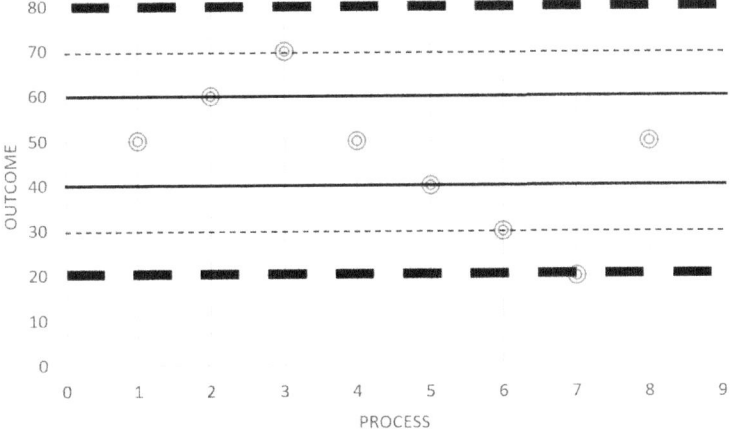

Figure 49: Process Ranges

Now you have four possible types of outcomes:

- The process is working ideally (within the solid inner lines).
- The process has a little more variation in outcomes (the small dotted line). In that case, intervene after 1.2 periods.
- The process has more variation in outcomes (the thick dashed line). In that case, intervene after 0.5 periods.
- The other option is to intervene immediately when the outcome falls outside of the thick dashed line.

Typically, quality control takes hold in a company in two to five years, creating quality circles concepts. Each team sets tighter objectives and tries to determine the improvement required based on incidents and feedback.

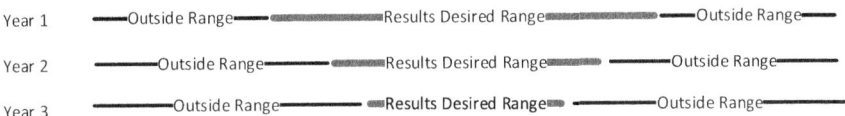

Figure 50: Quality Circle Concept

Let's draw a very simplified example. Measure the results of the outcomes in the process, and place the results as a dot on top of each other, leading to the following shape.

Figure 51: Data Points

This is called normal distribution; you can draw a bell shape on top of it. This means your results are on target and relatively predictable in range.

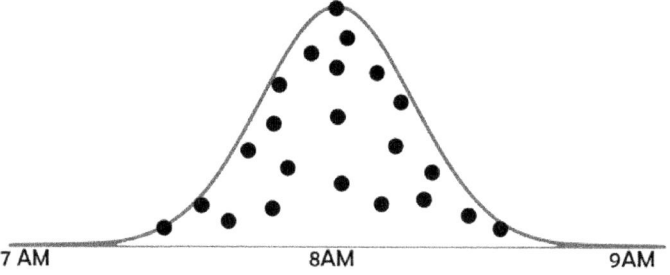

Figure 52: Normal Distribution

The mean is in the middle, which is at 8 a.m., the total points of the results are between 7:15 a.m. and 8:45 a.m.

The regular distribution must be a symmetrical bell-shaped curve; the bell cuts off at three standard deviations from the mean. Since we know that the three standard deviations are 45 minutes, this means that one standard deviation is equal to 15 minutes.

- Of the results, 99.7 percent are ±3 standard deviations from the mean
- Of the results, 95.4 percent are ±2 standard deviations from the mean
- Of the results, 68.2 percent are ±1 standard deviation from the mean

The defects are not about the final results only, but the possibility of final results. Let's compare two actions: making a cup of coffee and fixing a laptop or server.

How many moving parts exist? How many scenarios are there where things go wrong? The more possibilities for failure, the more difficult it will be to control the process. This is why we will discuss automation and how to make process chains shorter later on.

This is called defects per opportunity (DPO). It is expressed as

possibilities for defects / maximum possibilities for defects = DPO

This will show the efficiency of a department, so don't count the variations only. Always get the DPO.

Six Sigma

Six Sigma is a process that focuses on developing and delivering near-perfect products and services through using management strategies with statistical tools. The failure rate in Six Sigma is 3.4 defects in a million; that is the DPO. A defect in the Six Sigma world means unwanted results, whether it's a process outcome or a product. Usually, the Six Sigma project spans years and is applied only to critical processes that could damage the organization somehow if the process failed. Six Sigma is trying to control the three factors—time, cost, and quality—although it could be applied to only one of the three. I tried to simplify the process to be adapted and generate results faster.

The Six Sigma steps are listed below:

1. Define
2. Measure (data must be gathered to determine the response)
3. Analyze (identify the likely cause of the defect)
4. Improve the process to reduce the possibility or eliminate the cause
5. Control (monitor to maintain the levels)

Define phase: Define the project

Every requirement you need to put is in "critical to quality (CTQ)" parameters. The following bullet points translate the customer requirements. Then we transfer it to measurements (for example, intact delivery within 30 minutes). This means you need to define the circles of quality based on numbers.

Each of these needs a number relevant to the service or product the company is producing. Each one is used to define the shape of the bell curve.

The Measure of Central Tendency (Where Sample Is Centered)

- Mean (total / N)
- Median (central point in a range of arranged points from a set of data)
- Mode (the most frequently occurring value)

Measures of Spread (Dispersion)

- Range (difference between largest and smallest value)
- Deviation (how far the data point is from the mean [data – mean] must = 0
- Variance (to avoid the sum of the deviation to 0 issues, we square it first before the sum process, then divide it by n – 1 to get the variance)
- Standard deviation (the variance square root)

Process Performance Metrics

- Defects per unit (DPU) – things that can go wrong
- Defects per opportunity (DPO), stated as

    (defects detected / total possible defects) = DPO

- defects per million opportunities (DPMO), stated as

    DPO x 1 million = DPMO

- Rolled throughput yield (RTY): if there are ten processes, each with a success rate of 95 percent, multiply resulting in 59.8 percent, a very poor result.
- Cost of quality (COQ): cost of prevention, cost of inspection, cost of failure within the organization, external failures, warranty claims
- Cost of poor quality (COPQ): a matrix that includes the cost of internal failures, external failures, appraisal

Measure

In this step, collect the data mentioned in the defining phase. This will require modifying the application to insert the start and end time of a specific task to measure the duration to produce the results and/or measure the quality of the final product or service.

Typically we start with time, the easiest of the three governing factors (time, cost, quality) to control. Then we move into controlling cost and quality.

The sample strategy should be random (meaning every item can be chosen) and representative (meaning the selected items represent the entire group). Here are some guidelines:

- Avoid judgment sampling (based on opinion)
- Avoid convenience sampling (not representative of the whole)
- Use simple random sampling (a lottery)
- Use stratified random sampling (ensure the number selected from each group represents this group size)

Analysis

In the analysis phase, analyze the relationship between elements in the process to understand how changes to one thing will impact the others. To do that, measure the correlation.

Correlation is the relation between two things, either negative or positive. The measurement for this is called the correlation coefficient. It ranges from −1 to +1. If there is no correlation, it will be 0 or close to 0. If the two values increase together, it is considered a positive correlation. If one increases as the other decreases, it is considered a negative correlation.

Once the correlation between elements in the process is determined, use a Pareto chart to measure the number of defects. This is based on the 80/20 rule, so pick the top 20 percent (or less) to improve.

Improve Phase

Mistake-proofing prevents errors from occurring in the first place, minimizes errors, and detects errors immediately.

Collecting the voice of the customer is very important. Apply advanced techniques such as the net promoter score.

Surveys are not an accurate way of measuring users' satisfaction. No one will fill out a survey unless they are super dissatisfied or delighted.

Interviews will draw the same limited participation as surveys, so the results will be skewed.

Observation can change the behavior of the person being observed, which will also make the data invalid. This is why techniques like a mystery shopper are required to collect feedback.

Handouts (the process jump from one actor or owner to another is considered a problem since this is the most probable cause for things to fall into the cracks and become lost.

Decide on the Limits

Determine the factors and the variables in the process. This means what will impact the process positively or negatively, then list all factors. For each variable, create a high level and a low level. It cannot be more than X and cannot be less than Y.

It's a matter of probability of outcomes. Since you have two levels, your N is two. You have different numbers of variables called K, and final outcomes will be N to the power of K (N^K), so if we have two levels and three variables, this will give us eight (2^3) possible scenarios to run to find the best option. The best option is not necessarily the lowest number. The lowest number could generate a hidden effect that will impact the business negatively. So select the best option for the business by running simulations and deciding which one produces better results.

Control Plans

The control plan is a two-step process:

- Build SPC charts
- Build plans to fix the process if the process falls out of control

Build SPC Charts

There are two types of variation:

- **Random variation:** due to chance or common causes (such as poor design, bad methods, lack of training or supervision)
- **Nonrandom variation:** sporadic, special causes (such as jammed equipment, broken tools, untrained temp worker)

The control chart has the mean in the middle plus or minus the standard deviation required in Six Sigma (the standard deviation calculated earlier). The process doesn't have to go all the way to six sigmas; it could be satisfied with only two sigmas.

SPC has nothing to do with customer requirements; it's not the management requirements. It is purely statistical charts from the process's mean.

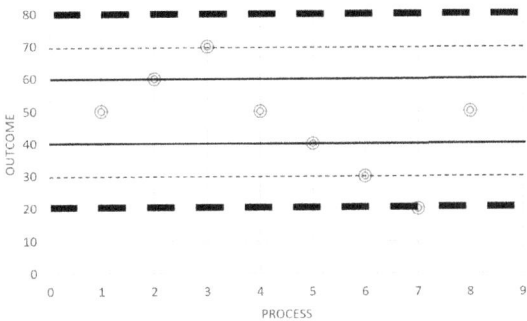

Figure 53: SPC Chart

There will be always random results in control charts, to determine if this is random or out of control conditions

- nine points in a row on the same side of the control line
- six points in a row, all increasing or decreasing

- fourteen points in a row alternating up and down
- two out of three points more than two standard deviations from the centerline
- four out of five points more than one standard deviation from the centerline
- fifteen successive points one standard deviation from the centerline
- eight successive points more than one standard deviation from the centerline

Chapter 10: Process as a Strategic Asset

A process is a set of activities to take a specific input and generate a specific output. If done properly, it will result in operations standardization, which will lead to better organization capability. Better organization capability leads to predictable revenues. The process needs to be leaner and performed with higher speed and quality to improve the revenue. Not only that, the process needs to evolve to stay relevant to the market.

The first step to understanding the process is that not all processes are the same. The organization has different levels and types of processes. Turning a process into an asset is a six-step process.

Step 1: Identify the process type and levels.

Step 2: Define the critical path.

Step 3: Give weight to the steps.

Step 4: Build service maps.

Step 5: Shorten the chain.

Step 6: Make use of robots.

Step 1: Identify the Process Type and Levels

Let's start with the types first.

Long: A process that generates customer value at the end of the process and typically has a long chain

Short: A process that generates an output that could be used by other processes and doesn't present direct customer value

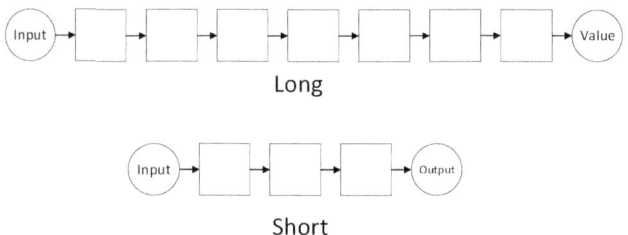

Figure 54: Process Types

And the levels of the processes functions are as follows:

Operational: Used to generate one specific output, such as password reset, new employee, or add to cart

Governing: Concerned with quality management, securing budget, planning, and monitoring. Typically this process produces a report at the end.

Tactical: A process that orchestrates other processes to generate the desired business result, for example, the complete cycle from the customer's arrival at the site to order fulfillment

Mixing both types and levels, you will end up with a matrix that looks like this:

	Operational	Governing	Tactical
Long			
Short			

Table 24 Process Distribution

Step 2: Define the Critical Path

Usually, organizations have hundreds of processes, if not thousands.

Some processes directly generate business value (revenue), and some processes are used internally to drive the business to function.

Business Analysis Techniques and Business Process Improvement | 143

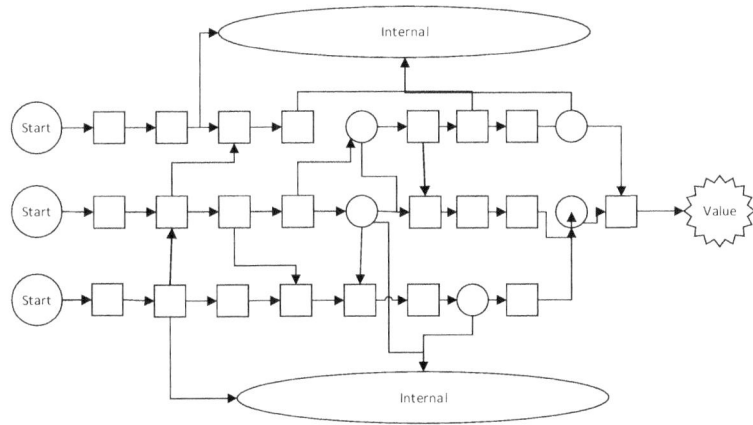

Figure 55: Process Map

The idea is to highlight the process chain that results in this value creation, the critical path, without which the business will simply stop, and revenue will halt. The removal of any process usually will cause such an impact, but we need to prioritize which process areas are the most valuable to the business and will have an immediate impact on the bottom line.

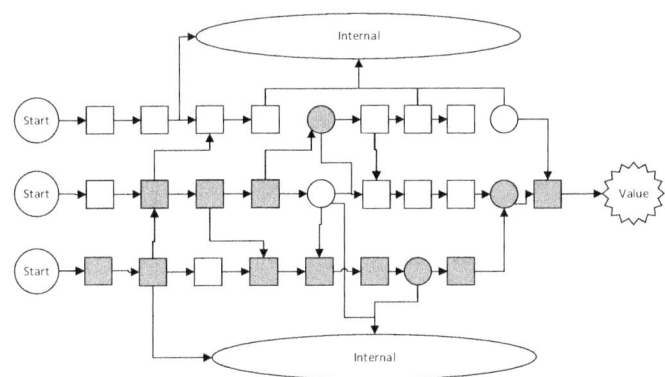

Figure 56: Process Critical Map

The impact goes tactical, operational, then governing. Generating a list of the most critical ones should not be difficult because you can track the money coming into the organization, so start at the end and work backward to the start.

Step 3: Give Weight to the Steps

Once the process list is ready, start building a map. The reason for this map is to define the process value to the business and show the value of IT. So the concern is with the process that generates value (the darker shade in Figure 57).

From this knowledge, move up in detail a level or two until you reach a block-based process that generates revenue for the business directly.

Take the blocks and give them a weight of contribution to the process itself.

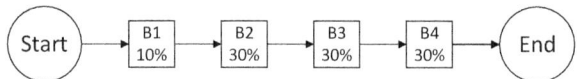

Figure 57: Process Contribution

Base the weight on the number of activities inside each building block or on the time it takes to finish this group of activities. This is a starting point on each building block contribution to the process.

This step aims to weight the benefits of optimization later on with the value returned from this change. Multiplying the blocks and the revenue generated from the process will lead to the value identification of this specific segment.

Step 4: Build Service Maps

The part aims to identify IT components with the revenue generated from this process, giving these parts more focus and attention and identifying things like disaster recovery, business continuity, and security scenarios later on.

Take the building blocks drawing and expand on it in two ways:

- **Upward**: Define the owners of the practice/block/process
- **Downward**: Identify the overall system, the other blocks dependent on it

Business Analysis Techniques and Business Process Improvement | 145

Build a service map. Start with the process owners at the very top, next to the block owner(s), and keep drilling down through all the layers of the IT.

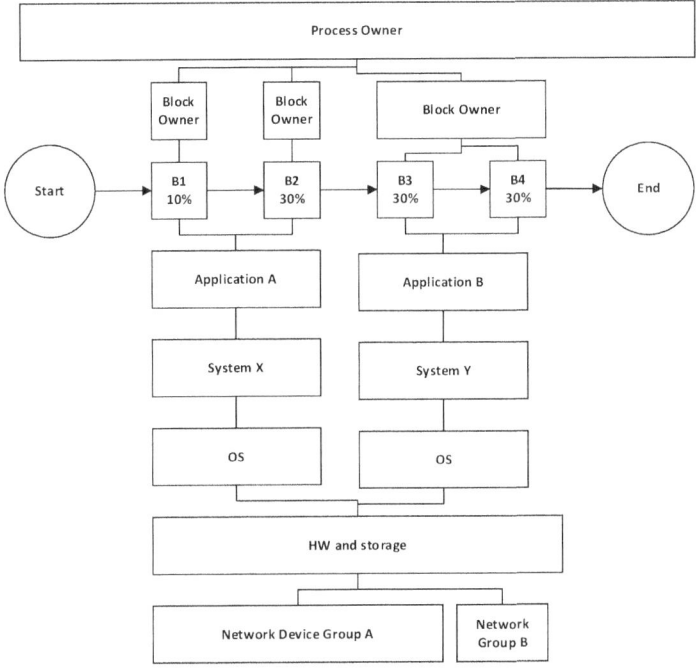

Figure 58: Process Owners

This will allow you to assess the impact of the change in the next steps. For example, Application B impacts 60 percent of the process, while Application A impacts 40 percent. This could be a prioritization schema to select which system to upgrade and optimize next.

Step 5: Shorten the Chain

At this point, there should be full visibility over the process. Now it's time to optimize it further. The first step, of course, is the tactical processes, as mentioned earlier.

Push every type of process down. Make the long into short and the short into automated.

	Operational	Governing	Tactical
Long			
Short			
Automated			

Table 25 Move the Process

Typically companies automate the operational processes first because they are the easiest to automate. The problem is that most of the revenue-generating process is tactical, so it's quite difficult to tie operational processes to the organization's bottom line. Therefore, the tactical transformation will be in two steps.

Step 5A: Find a way to break a long process into multiple processes with exact input and output. This means a new process owner, new flowcharts, etc.

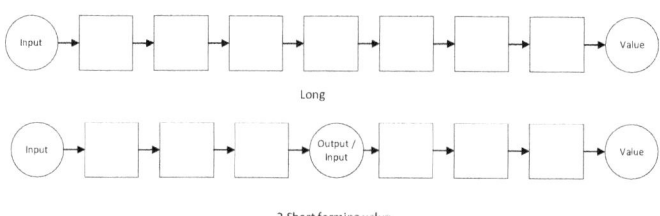

Figure 59: Process Split

Step 5B: Automate parts of the chain to produce value to the business faster through faster order fulfillment, faster checkout process, faster support services. This will digitally transform the process and improve the business for operational excellence.

Step 6: Make Use of Robots

The technology landscape is ever-growing; no day goes by without some startup releasing software to the public and increasing the complication of the software landscape. The solution is automation.

This results in many software packages in your day-to-day operations, many of which don't communicate well or don't have the necessary built-in automation to perform certain tasks when specific conditions are met. This leads to employees spending long hours performing basic repetitive tasks or waiting for X output to start Y action.

Let's analyze this further, looking at what workers in an organization normally do:

- Move basic data
- Enter data
- Make decisions
- Analyze information
- Respond to requests
- Collect data and respond
- Innovate
- Learn
- Test
- Use audio/visual recognition
- Measure
- Coordinate with others
- Adapt to the situation based on history
- Offer feedback of the situation

This is only a sample of the most common actions a traditional office worker does in day-to-day operations. The objective is to see time-wasting activities and plan to replace them with something else.

Figure 61: Traditional Worker Tasks

In each process, the first action is to determine three things:

- repetitiveness of the activity
- frequency of the activity
- duration of single activity

The next step is to identify the activity as rule-based or decision-based.

A decision-based activity requires human cognitive ability to analyze and decide on a problem or any creativity.

A rule-based activity is defined based on specific parameters that decide the output of the activity.

Usually, the more the activity is based on decision, the more it will be passed on to a person (not even AI can do that), but the more you can switch processes from decisions-based to rule-based, the more possibilities you have to automate them.

When starting out based on employee descriptions, the majority will be decision-based systems. The challenge is to convert these to rule-based and make them a standard of operation before implementing robotic process automation (RPA).

What stops the conversion might be inputs of the process that need to be standardized to ensure that a business rule can run effectively, for example, accepting the input as an .xml or .csv file with a specific structure to be processed. Another challenging area of RPA is standardizing the process itself to ensure it can shift from decision-based to rule-based.

Usually, a very small subset of an organization is rule-based unless the organization is a highly regulated setup such as the financial sector. The business objective is to define the candidate for RPA, standardize the process, ensure the rule can be applied, and then switch to automation project.

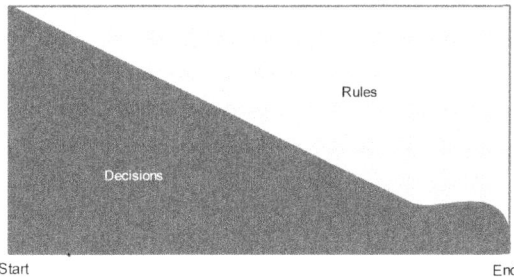

Figure 62: Activity Types

These factors will prioritize what to transform. Let's take a simple example: a support agent. It is possible to augment the support agent process of incident resolution and customer service by using a chat agent. The robot would solve an issue automatically, but it will move to the agent if it fails.

The human agent will have all the data collected by the chat robot, an AI-suggested list of possible solutions, and additional information collected from the history of the customer or user.

As shown in the example, the automation could be two levels:

- Augmenting and supporting the current agents to perform better
- Replacing parts of the process or entire process

Combining both methods, as in the example, helps to deliver more optimized results. The goal is to give the business the time required to perform other activities that cannot be transformed to automation.

There is one dangerous assumption. The labor market has a shortage of skills required to operate the business, which is true in many parts of the world. But in some areas, it is not. Let me put this another way: If your resources are not loaded with work, they have lots of free time. Automation will be a waste because simply adding to their free time will not produce value. It's possible for a process to stop at the switch from decision-based to rule-based.

Though there are other reasons an activity should be automated, not all good automation candidates should be switched over to full automation. Automation has costs as well, and its cost might exceed the cost of the traditional system.

Automation

There are Four types of automation:

- **Scripting-based**: A script that does a specific function, like a micro in Microsoft Office application
- **Runbook automation**: A series of steps and rules of "If X then Y" that follows a serial sequence and typically is based on scripts running on the systems
- **Robotic process automation**
- **Application refactoring**: Rewritten application code to include automation

Business Analysis Techniques and Business Process Improvement | 151

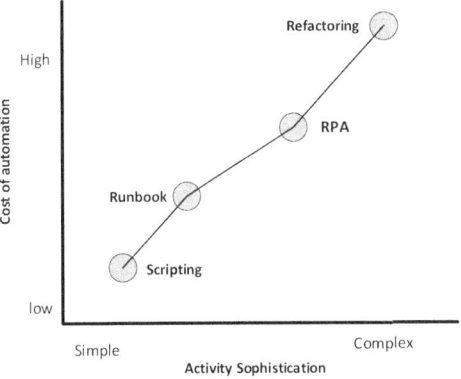

Figure 63: Automation Options

Robotic Process Automation (RPA)

RPA is a software tool with both business rules and a sequence of actions that follows the if-then type. Some tools can mimic the human behavior of clicks to automate the tasks (not API Integration).

The difference between RPA and runbook automation (RBA) (orchestration) is that RPA has one extra element: business rules.

A business rule is a rule coming from the business, not from the IT that governs some aspect of the task. For example, withdrawal limits at an ATM are based on card type and customer level, and the issuing bank. The rule has nothing to do with the operation of the withdrawal itself, but it's enforced to ensure compliance with the predefined rule.

There is something in between, but it's not server-based. It's desktop-based, and it's called robotic desktop automation (RDA). It's the same concept as a script or a macro; it's a set of actions or a workflow triggered by a person to perform a predefined series of tasks to assist them in their daily work.

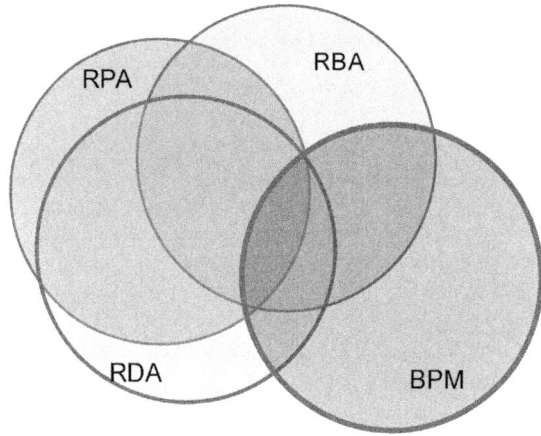

Figure 64: Process Domain

To build an action plan, develop the process maps first to measure the best candidates for the automation with the highest return on investment (ROI). Once you do that, the tool comes into effect, building the robot that will do the function.

Reasons for RPA Project

- Increase the speed of a specific task without compromising the integrity of the business rules
- Ensure compliance with particular rules
- Free people from routine tasks to focus on more critical tasks
- Achieve consistency in results, leading to more optimized process and overall quality improvement
- Eliminate specific jobs and repurpose employees for other tasks

The number of reports implemented is not the measure of success. Still, the ROI is the key to determining the business value, so always tie the project objectives to business value, not technical terms.

Printed in Great Britain
by Amazon